AF482512

A word to the readers

We do not know what is happening to us, and this is precisely what is happening to us, not to know what is happening to us
José Ortega y Gasset

Human today has fallen into a terrible fire, which is called Alienation. Self-forgetfulness causes human to give up loving himself and not discover a reason for his existence. When he cannot discover the cause of his own existence, at certain moments he engages in actions that are often unintentionally anti-human. He does not know what action he is taking and he does not know whether this action was right or wrong in a situation where society has led human to depoliticize. He only acts and finds no reason for his actions. With a logic that considers truth dead and completely relativistic, that person will be more likely to justify his actions and will not seek the truth at all, or anything close to the truth. Human will not understand himself until he seeks to discover the closest thing to the truth, and human who does not know his individual identity will have no understanding of collective identity and Otherness. There is a close relationship between identity and truth. Without identity, there is no truth, and where there is no truth, anonymity shows itself.

The way forward for human is to think about the self. By looking at history, by taking refuge in art, by understanding philosophy, by perusing mythology and cultures, human can see his true face in the mirror and visualize another in the mirror.

The aim of Hermes Magazine is to present beauty and glory to its audience in the form of words, and by publishing the different ideas of writers from different countries and cultures, to some extent represent the true nature of human societies. We are very happy that you are the reader of this magazine and you are following us.

YOUR FRIEND,

Mohammad Abedi

Contents

Philosophy

Mythology

Literature

Art History

Other Articles

Poetry

Short Story

PHILOSOPHY

VIOLENCE AND POVERTY

BY THOMAS POGGE

Violence and avoidable poverty are the two cardinal evils of human history. They stand out because they are human-made: they are evils humanity inflicts upon itself or, more accurately, evils that human beings inflict on one another. They stand out also because each of them destroys vastly more human potential than natural calamities, such as diseases and natural catastrophes, whose effects they hugely magnify in any case.

Violence and avoidable poverty are the greatest challenges in our struggle to maintain faith in humanity. Many have lost this faith forever in the face of the slave trade, the Holocaust, the devastation of Vietnam, the genocide in Rwanda, or the ongoing massive deprivations imposed upon the world's poor: from starvation to human trafficking. Freedom from violence and poverty are central to our otherwise diverse dreams of a redeeming human future, in which no child's physical and mental development is stunted by malnutrition, forced labor or air pollution, in which no woman is subservient from fear of destitution or beatings, in which – forever safe from violence and poverty – all human beings can freely develop and express themselves, can freely cultivate and contribute their skills and talents.

In working toward a world without violence and poverty, we should seek to understand why violence and poverty persist on such a massive scale. We know how to resolve conflicting claims on the basis of standing rules, democratically adopted and impartially adjudicated by an independent professional judiciary. The domestic lives of many national societies demonstrate this know-how, showing that large numbers of people can form a lively and diverse political community in which violence and the capacity for violence have lost all importance. So why are we not globalizing this know-how, why don't we resolve international conflicts in the way we resolve – in the more progressive countries, at least – intra-national conflicts?

Some of these same progressive societies also illustrate that we know how to banish poverty. The world is easily rich enough to avoid all human destitution. This is possible even with just a mildly more equal distribution of existing income and wealth. Currently, the gross world product – the market value of all the goods and services humanity produces in a year, converted at purchasing power – is USD 50 per person per day. In such a world, why should anyone have to live below USD 10 per day? Yet, fully 3 out of 8 billion human beings cannot afford the even substantially lower cost of a healthy diet – and this figure is from 2019, even before the COVID-19 pandemic struck.[1]. Some 2.368 billion human beings are food insecure, living on about USD 4 or less.[2]. The World Health Organization reports that "globally, at least 2 billion people use a drinking

----

[1] FAO, IFAD, UNICEF, WFP and WHO (2021). The State of Food Security and Nutrition in the World 2021. Transforming food systems for food security, improved nutrition and affordable healthy diets for all. FAO. https://doi.org/10.4060/cb4474en, p.27.

[2] Ibid., p. 18. This 2020 figure has been increasing each and every year since 2014.

water source contaminated with faeces,"[3] that "2.0 billion people still do not have basic sanitation facilities such as toilets or latrines,"[4] and that "an estimated two billion people have no access to essential medicines, effectively shutting them off from the benefits of advances in modern science and medicine."[5] UN Habitat reports that "more than 1.8 billion people worldwide lack adequate housing."[6].

The heavily dominant richest 5% of humanity appropriate 40% of the gross world product and leave 5% of it for the poorest 50%.[7]. An institutional shift of just 5% of gross world product from the former segment to the latter could end all severe poverty without serious cost to anyone. Wealth inequality is even much more extreme, with the richest 1.1% of humanity owning nearly half of all household wealth worldwide and the poorest 55% owning merely 1.3%.[8]. This oppressive impoverishment of the poorer half also manifests itself in large disparities in education, health and longevity.[9]. Roughly 30% of all human deaths are premature from poverty-related causes.[10].

Averting destitution would be even easier in the vastly richer world that we would have if we abolished violence and poverty. Just think of all the economic destruction caused by violence and all the waste caused by the endless preparations for violence. Think of all the economic losses that result when poverty prevents human beings from reaching their potential: when undernourishment stunts their mental and physical development, when lack of education and continuous privation diminish their contributions to society.

If a world without violence and poverty is so clearly possible, then what is holding us back? What are the political forces that prevent us from making steady progress toward such a world?

To answer this question, we must understand the basics of political power. Political power derives from three main sources: military might, the capacity to hurt and kill and thus to coerce other people; economic strength, the capacity to control essential resources and thereby other people and their services; plus, a residual category of "soft power," which includes cultural influence, charisma, moral reputation and the capacity to convince others by sound argument. In all three dimensions, power is relative: what matters is how much military might, wealth or soft power some political actor has relative to other political actors. Any political actor therefore has a fundamental interest in increasing its relative standing in each of the three dimensions. But such an increase typically comes at a cost in other dimensions: by purchasing a new

----

[3] https://www.who.int/news-room/fact-sheets/detail/drinking-water.

[4] https://www.who.int/news-room/fact-sheets/detail/sanitation.

[5] https://www.who.int/publications/10-year-review/chapter-medicines.pdf.

[6] https://unhabitat.org/programme/housing-rights.

[7] Data for 2019 kindly provided by Branko Milanovic (personal communication).

[8] Shorrocks, A., Davies, J., & Lluberas, R. (2021). Global Wealth Report 2021. Credit Suisse Research Institute. https://www.credit-suisse.com/about-us/en/reports-research/global-wealth-report.html, p. 17. The world's 2,755 billionaires own about three times as much wealth as the entire poorer half of humanity (https://www.forbes.com/billionaires). The income and wealth percentages in this paragraph are calculated on the basis of current foreign exchange rates.

[9] Life expectancy varies greatly by country, from 85 in Hong Kong and Japan to 55 is the Central African Republic – with Iran at 77. See https://www.worldometers.info/demographics/life-expectancy.

[10] Worldwide poverty is the focus of a new journal – Academics Stand Against Poverty – which has just published its inaugural issue (http://journalasap.org/index.php/asap). Its central aim is to support the understanding and eradication of poverty.

weapons system, a state is increasing its military might but also reducing its economic might. By invading a neutral country, a state may improve its military position, but at the cost of diminishing its moral standing. By providing foreign aid, a state may increase its soft power while reducing its economic strength. We can think of such moves as prudential conversions of one kind of political power into another. Such conversions are possible, but only to a limited extent.

Our dream of a world without violence and poverty is the dream of a world in which military might is no longer a significant source of political power. This marginalization of the capacity for violence has already been achieved within many countries, where the physical strength of politicians, or the weapons possessed by them or their bodyguards, play no role in political contestations. Our dream of a world without violence and poverty is also the dream of a world in which economic might – income and wealth – are much more equally distributed and for this reason likewise of diminished importance. When economic inequalities are small, then the rich cannot dominate and oppress the poor. Moreover, when economic inequalities are small, then the interests of the rich in regard to the design of the economic and political system are not so different from the interests of the poor, so that the rich have not merely lesser opportunities but also weaker incentives to use their economic might to push for institutional arrangements more favorable to themselves. Our dream of a world without violence and poverty is then the dream of a world in which political conflicts are resolved mainly through the strength of arguments, through the capacity to convince others about which political decisions would best promote justice and the common good.

Who could be against such a world? The answer is evident: those who currently have a lot of political power that is mainly based on military might or economic might or both. The reason is this. How much each of the three sources contributes to overall political power is context-dependent. In contexts of war or belligerent tensions and hostilities, the military component of political power is most important and the capacity for moral wisdom and convincing reasoning has little importance or none at all (as expressed in Stalin's famous interjection: "The Pope! How many divisions does he have?"). By contrast, in a peaceful and harmonious setting, the capacity for violence contributes nothing or very little to an actor's political power, and its capacity for reasonable and convincing argument contributes a lot. It follows that power-maximizing actors who have a comparative advantage in military might have a systematic interest in influencing the general environment toward tension and hostility, whereas power-maximizing actors with a comparative advantage in reasonable argument have a systematic interest in influencing the general environment toward harmony and mutual respect.

The notion of "comparative advantage" indicates a double relativity: to the other dimensions of an actor's political power and to the actor's competitors. Thus, that an actor has a comparative advantage in military might means that, among its peers or rivals, its military ranking is higher than its economic and soft-power ranking. This actor may be superior to its competitors in all three dimensions; but it is more superior militarily. In our world, the key states with a comparative advantage in military might are the United States and Russia. Their international military standing exceeds their standing in the other two dimensions, and they both therefore benefit from a geopolitical environment characterized by belligerence, tensions and hostilities. Such an environment requires no open warfare; it requires that war is an ever-present possibility and that violence flares up here and there as a reminder of the continuing importance of military capabilities.

A state with a comparative advantage in military might benefits from a global climate of tensions and hostilities in which its military strength commands deference from others with concession of special privileges that would otherwise be indefensible. This benefit is especially important to the leader of such a state's executive branch, because a climate of tensions and hostilities enhances not merely his state's power relative to other states, but also his own domestic power relative to the other branches of government and relative to any politically significant popular movements. If somehow violence became impossible, the Presidents of Russia and the U.S. would be the greatest losers, finding their political power drastically diminished – because their states would lose power internationally, and because their offices would lose power within those states.

What about political actors whose comparative advantage lies in economic might? They may have an interest in averting open warfare that would render their wealth insecure. But they also have a systematic interest in an environment characterized by tensions and hostilities, for two reasons. First, military might depends on economic strength, and those who possess economic strength can convert it into military might or use it to influence those with military might. Second, a climate of tensions and hostilities sidelines moral concerns and specifically moral challenges to large economic inequalities, severe poverty, economic oppression and exploitation. International tensions and hostilities make it easy for the rich to declare the world to be a jungle in which they can ill afford the luxury of morality. One often hears such arguments from and within affluent states: that in the jungle of international relations we cannot afford to treat weaker states and their populations decently because in doing so we would weaken ourselves in the all-important competition with one's strongest rivals or adversaries, who are heavily armed and prone to exploit any weakness we may show.

The high degree of latent violence in our world helps uphold then its horrendous economic injustices against the poor – injustices that would be condemned as plainly indefensible in any reasonable moral debate: the injustice of air pollution and greenhouse gas emissions, the injustice of extortionate intellectual property rights, the injustice of agricultural protectionism, the injustice of overt and covert violent interventions, the injustice of spyware and social-media manipulation, the injustice of bribery and corruption of public officials, the injustice of tax havens, the injustice of extracting repayment of debts incurred by illegitimate autocrats, and the injustice of natural resources exported against payment made to rulers who lack support and authorization from "their" people. All these everyday injustices are ones that benefit the big multinational corporations, banks, hedge funds, billionaires, corrupt and captured politicians who, insofar as they have an interest in maintaining these injustices, have an interest in the continuation of our world as one in which violence is an ever-present threat.

To conclude. The transition toward a world of peace and reasoned discource would bring enormous collective gains for humankind and would benefit the vast majority of human beings. Only the interests of a tiny minority are systematically opposed. But this tiny minority is very powerful in the world as it is. And this minority enjoys the further advantage that it is far easier to create than to preempt crises, far easier to drive up tensions and hostilities than to drive them down.

Nonetheless, I am cautiously optimistic that the needed transition can be achieved. Even members of the tiny global "elite" can see that humankind will not survive for long if we stay with the present paradigm. Gorbachev saw this clearly, and he was willing to use his political power, to use up his political power, in a brave and yet failed effort to progress the needed transition. Moreover, the world's people can learn to better understand the deep, systematic root of the persistence of violence and poverty in so many parts of the world, and they may then collaborate across national borders to press for the needed political changes in the global institutional architecture: against unilateral military interventions, for a world parliament, and for an organization of the world economy that secures a fair share of the global social product for every human being. We must of course also oppose violence and heal its scars locally. But we will never remove the need for these good efforts unless we also reform the deep structural causes of violence and injustice, which are related to the extraordinary political power they secure for a small elite.

FORTUNE IN RELIGION, AND PHILOSOPHY FROM THE MIDDLE AGES TO THE MODERN DAY

BY MADILYN GRACE PHELPS

First introduced by the Roman senator Boethius (477-524 AD) in his seminal work The Consolation of Philosophy, the concept of fortune became a lasting influence in theology and philosophy. As both fields delve into greater mysteries in life and how to practice good sense and overcome adversity, fortune has been treated as both a fickle beast and as a worthy circumstance to be earned. Universally, fortune's place in society is to name the forces in life we have no control over. Over time, fortune's mystical connotations have evolved into a secular usage to accept said loss of control in a stoic bid to rise above challenges.

Finding its origins in the goddess Fortuna, fortune reached its most potent metaphor in The Fortune's Wheel (Rota Fortunae) written in The Consolation of Philosophy. In it, Fortune functions as a wheel and wherever one finds oneself, crushed on the bottom or at the very top, is a commentary on how one gets there. In the earliest ideas of moral teachings, they were based in one's own conduct. Similar to the oft touted concept of "karma," when one finds themselves in unfortunate circumstances the determination was that they must have done something to deserve it. On the other end of the spectrum, when one's circumstances are good, they ware worthy in the eyes of the dealings of fortune. What makes fortune interesting is that the usage does not have to be specifically theological. As religious practices changed and evolved, the concept of fortune evolved into the ideas of fate and luck. These are decidedly abstract and used in the most innocuous of situations.

Medieval writer Christine de Pizan wrote, "Whatever then may be your state, by Fortune who controls your fate, govern yourself in such a way that good sense will there hold sway.[1]. Nicolo Machiavelli wrote "He who has relied on Fortune less has maintained his position best."[2]. In both examples form vastly different genres, the authors acknowledge Fortune as being something of an unreliable element. Those who rely on it too much are bound to suffer. From religious instruction to Chaucer, Arthurian romances to Shakespeare, to "Mirrors for Princes" genre of political philosophy, the early examples of fortune are clearly focused a practical usage of fortune's circumstances and how to cultivate good fortune and avoid the bad fortunes. This is true to an extent because as we know, success is not always guaranteed through hard work and dedication. Cultivating good relations, wealth and accident of birth also greatly contribute to the outward success or otherwise in one's life.

"Outward success" is emphasized because part of the practice of philosophy is cultivating inner goodness, satisfaction, and assurance of how one is responsible for one's own actions in an uncertain world. This is the basis of Stoic philosophy, where the likes of Seneca and Epictetus both had much to say on fortune. They acknowledge that capricious nature, as well as the necessity to use your circumstances to do the most good for yourself and practice at overcoming the whims of fortune.

Like many ancient and abstract concepts, it made its way into books and songs in the modern world. These days, it is called Lady Luck or fate. That phrase "Everything happens for a reason" is one that alludes to a predestined fortune. In addition to showing how ancient our earliest teachings are, it demonstrates how people are still feeling out of control or seeking it. Fortune's Wheel is a great metaphor to apply one's circumstances and set as a standard to keep. Bad fortunes, or the threat of bad fortunes, was often a reason for the cultivation of good fortune.

Fortune and its Wheel have survived beyond its clever usage as a metaphor for good luck and bad luck. It teaches us that other than our own actions, there is not much else we are truly responsible for. Time spent worrying about things out of our control could take time away from doing good for one's own self and for others. These stoic philosophers, priests and chroniclers use fortune to instruct those afraid and uncertain in their lives to do what you can with what you have and approach life fearlessly, meeting abstract challenge and mortal foe alike head on.

Rota Fortunae, found in Bocaccio's "De Casibus Virorum Illustrium (On the Fates of Famous Men)," 1467.

https://www.gla.ac.uk/myglasgow/library/files/special/exhibns/month/feb2009.html

MULTI-PURPOSE SOCIETY AS A FACTOR OF GLOBAL SOCIO-CULTURAL CHANGE

BY DOROTA OKRASIŃSKA

Abstract:

On the way of contemporary economic transformations the semiotics of productivity seems to refer to the field of globalization. The society adapted to life in the spirit of "multi-purpose effect" in every professional and social situation makes a choice and consent to fit into the canons of satisfying social needs without a sense of limit. Through collective consent, it becomes the rule to perform multiple functions and professional positions in a single job or to integrate several disciplines into a single department. The shallowing of specialization and the ignoring of individual competence are only the beginning of the transformation of thought. At the same time, on a personal level, the notion of balance and moderation is being narrowed by extending priorities to include the number of tasks to be performed at the highest level. In such an illusory functionalist society, every citizen appears to be maximally efficient, perfect and time-managed.

Model employee, husband, father, gamer, cook, driver, expert, "golden handyman" are just some of the roles and patches that contribute to the social pressure to strive for the ideal model. In this way, reflection over the hierarchy of performed tasks as well as their quality disappears. Similarly, the multiplicity of fulfilled roles requires verification, as a result of which it is worth asking a question whether a human being as an individual does not impose too many functions on himself/herself? It is also important to consider the causes and consequences of such a management model on a global level.

Keywords: multi-purpose, globalization, balance, deskilling.

Introduction

This article focuses on the concept of "multi-purpose effect" society. The phenomenon of multifunctional human performance management can be interchangeably referred to as multi-job, multi-time, multi-task and multi-functional. The multifaceted understanding of man as an expert in everything forces him to fit in with the current social standards. What follows is a race of roles, which are assigned not only by a given organization, but also by the community members themselves. Implementing the accepted roles requires performing functions that would normally be difficult to assign to oneself individually. So where does the conformist attitude towards assigned tasks come from?

Social mechanisms of "multi-purpose effect"

The theme of multifunctionality is related to the mechanisms of globalization. This process is responsible for the penetration of structures into the community (Okon-Horodyńska, 2007). There is then a gradual shift in the degree of sovereignty to the level of global systemic benefits. Social benefits are superficially formulated to arouse the individual's desire to possess and pursue multiple specific roles while strengthening the economy (e.g. pressure to have children, marry, study).

Social trust along with conformity in emerging processes is determined by individual predispositions, shaped by physical and behavioral factors as well as those resulting from organizational culture characteristics.

To take a closer look at physical factors, it is worth mentioning perseveration, which is described in more detail by S. Kowalik. According to this theory, if each person's stream of consciousness perceives and assimilates a predominantly uniform message, then the mind stops capturing other perspectives (Kowalik, 2015). Such narrowed perception options lead to the adoption of a paradigm as the only and universally acceptable one. The phenomenon of the so-called dopamine loop (compulsion loop) works in a similar way, resulting in the release of dopamine under the influence of an addictive factor (Brooks, 2011). In this case, the element compulsion may be the very act of remaining in the community in light of social expectations, norms, demands, and even pressures. It is also associated with a sense of social identity with the group (Okoń-Horodyńska, 2007). In this way, the created need distances from the ability to reflectively look at individual responsibilities or maintain life- and work-balance.

Referring to the area of identity, it is worth mentioning here the phenomenon of relativization, which imposes the treatment of an individual as an element of society (Okoń-Horodyńska, 2007:73). Gradual deprivation of individuality, inte- gration of the "I" with the group as a unity, leads to disintegration of personality.

In this way, society, on its way to achieving prosperity and well-being, sees the aspect of multifunctionality as an obligatory springboard to professional and private fulfillment.

Globalization and the loss of individual control

The subject of this analysis is not only the mechanism of the "multi-purpose effect" itself but also the question of the influence of organizational culture and globalization, on the processes occurring.

It is important to clarify the role of globalization. This phenomenon affects the entire structure of society, which translates into unreflective adaptation to prevailing trends and standards of work and life. Breaking out of the emerging patterns threatens the individual with marginalization (Kowalik, 2015).

A broader perspective in looking at the concept of globalization was presented by A. Jagoda, comparing a person in the trend of systemicity to an asset. (Jagoda, 2017:38). The author also draws attention to the phenomenon of deskilling, which leads to the replacement of human competencies with technologies or to stop at low-skilled staff in order to standardize requirements to the company's internal rules. As a result, corporations hire an employee for an extended position, which is occupied by one man, which can be referred to the archetypal figure - everyman from Franz Kafka's "The Trial" (Kafka, 2016). Using this perception as an example, an everyman could occupy certain positions where the competencies possessed or qualifications have little meaning, while rank is given to increased productivity.

Similar importance can be given to organizational culture. As R. Griffin points out, it represents a set of beliefs, values and symbols that shape the mood and behavior of the entire organization (Griffin, 2017: 448). Thus, an internally adopted system of rules often imposes the accepted perspective of action as the only valid strategy. An example can be given of a situation where a citizen as an employee is accepted to a certain position without precise arrangements about the competencies, abilities, preferences as well as the specifics of the field undertaken. A frequent practice becomes management by maximization, where the use of the employee's time is aimed at the complete management of his working time and personnel needs regardless of individual specialization. In this way, for example, an administrative employee is assigned tasks such as bookkeeping or reception, a teacher as a special educator, and a store clerk as a store clerk or supervisor. The lack of clear rules contributes to a disrupted sense of control over one's own life. This can result in frustration, stress, burnout or reduced ability to analyze due to overload of the body.

Similar phenomena occur in private life. Among the commonly accepted socio-cultural expectations in European culture, we can include exemplary goals:

- starting a family
- having a full-time job
- religious observance
- buying an apartment
- completing education
- study
- conforming to norms

It is worth noting that the cited examples impose social roles performed on a daily basis. Often these positions overlap, occurring at the same time (e.g. studying, working full-time at a complex job and starting a family), resulting in a loss of balance in personal life. Thus, the assumed roles build in a social aspect a number of material benefits for the state economy (tax revenues, support of university budgets, empowerment of educational institutions), which, however, is often in opposition to the balance of the individual. Condensed social expectations thus enforce behavior based on conformity to patterns. Each individual then strives to complete all roles as a priority, as quickly as possible to enhance the sense of empowerment.

Paradigm conflict in the context of change

The considerations undertaken draw attention to the importance of paradigms as a plane, a reference point for the perspectives adopted. According to this claim, they provide a space for the accumulation of concepts, values and viewpoints on which models of social behavior can be built (Kuhn, 2009).

In this aspect, we can distinguish a functionalist (systemic) paradigm based on building a sustainable system based on mutual cooperation. It is worth noting that this system treats holistically often only mass needs. Thus, building a system of structures is increasingly based on an excess of positions and roles to be fulfilled, which determines its maintenance. The model constructed in this way tends to satisfy the needs of the masses, while correspondingly, the needs of the individual as a personality become separated. The needs of the collective then assume the highest rank, gradually denying place to the needs of the individual. Desires for balance, development, individualism or a non-conformist way of life become limited. The system thus created appears to be an illusion of holistic order, because its foundations are based on schemes rather than competencies or attitudes.

The opposite of the example given is radical structuralism, which in practice proposes solutions to effect change. Restoring balance in the workplace, breaking patterns, cultivating competencies, respect for individual will, freedom, are the basic features of this approach (Szydło, 2014). The loosening of the prevailing structures here is fundamental to changing the accepted model of life. The fight against the domination of accepted forms or pluralism becomes an opportunity to break away from illusory structures.

Understanding the transformations as the "multi-effect purpose" process unfolds requires deep insight into an individual's goals. Reflection on proper prioritization of tasks, non-conformism, and awareness of what is necessary require self-discipline. The ability to manage one's own time seems to be an essential component of a new paradigm based on a real balance between different interest groups.

Reflection on contemporary processes of multi-purpose society leads to the conclusion that the implementation of assumed roles should be subject to reflection. Supporting individuality, subjectivity and sovereignty can be manifested by limiting social or professional pressure to perform imposed roles. It is also worth mentioning here about work on communication, which is a means of establishing an adequate position.

Summary

To summarize possible remedial solutions, it is fundamental to be aware of responsibility and choice in sustaining the trend of using human resources to the maximum. The right to make decisions is held by those who manage the work of others as well as by individuals. The same right applies to each person's personal life regardless of social patterns or pressures. Finding and nurturing one's own boundary in the way of personal time management becomes the overarching remedy. Discussion of these mechanisms has the potential to impact public health, job satisfaction and personal balance.

References

Brooks, R. (2011). Compulsion loops and dopamine hits How games are designed to be addictive. Obtained from: https://pl.gyoumagazine.com/article/compulsion_loops_and_dopamine_hits_how_games_are_de signed_to_be_addictive

Griffin, W. (2017). Fundamentals of organizational management. Warszawa: PWN, 448.

Jagoda, A. (2017). Work organization in the enterprise. Identification, diagnosis, perspectives. Wrocław: University of Economics, 38.

Kafka, F. (2016). The Trial. Łódź: Oficyna.

Okoń-Horodyńska, E. (2007). Man and society in the face of globalization. Economic Studies. Kraków: Jagiellonian University, 73.

Kowalik, S. (2019). A dormant society. Warszawa: Sedno.

Kuhn, T.S. (2009). The structure of scientific revolutions. Warszawa: Aletheia

Szydło, J. (2014). Paradigms of organizational culture. Economics and Managment, 4(2014).

MYTHOLOGY

SOL INVICTUS MITHRAS: A GLOBAL GOD IN THE ROMAN EMPIRE

BY MARICA FELICI

The Imperial Age of ancient Rome is traditionally considered to begin in 27 B.C.E., the first year of Octavian Augustus's Principate, and to end in 395 C.E. when, after the death of Theodosius I, the empire had been divided into two distinct parts, the Western Roman Empire, with the new capital based in Milan (and later Ravenna), and the Eastern Roman Empire, based in the first moment in Nicomedia, and later in Constantinople.

During the four centuries of its life, the Roman Empire came to extend its influence over regions that are today part of three different continents (Europe, Africa, and Asia Minor).   In this incredibly vast territory, interconnections of various nature are to be expected: one context of exchange and hybridization was the religious one.

In ancient Rome the religious system was profoundly intertwined with the political one, and it is impossible to understand one without considering the other. This discourse is valid even in the case of mysteries cults. These are secret cults distinct from the official public religion of the State and, even though we have a wide variety of different cults, they all share similar features: the most important one is that admission to the cult is restricted to initiates whom, after performing a secret ritual, become part of a group characterized by a set of understandings and knowledge not accessible to non-initiates. The main reason behind joining such cults was the salvation offered by being in service of a specific divinity: the salvation we are talking about could be of a practical nature – for example, the initiates could ask for having an illness cured – or it could be of a more spiritual one – and this is typical of mysteries cults from the first century C.E. onward: here, we are referring to the salvation of the soul after death.

The cult of the god Mithras encompasses all of the elements presented so far. As fascinating as it is, Mithraism is also a difficult cult to grasp because of the scarcity of sources: the literary and philosophical accounts are influenced by Stoic and Neoplatonic doctrines as well as by the Christian one, which describes the cult as false and diabolic. Nonetheless, we are able to reconstruct the main elements of the cult thanks to the abundance of mithraea – the places where the mysteries were performed –, which present fixed characteristics even though their topographic presence is widespread within the limes of the Roman Empire.

The presence of the god Mithras dates back to the Indo-European religions. In the Rg-Veda Mitra (as the name is spelled) is associated with the god Varuna, who is presented as the king among the gods, and whose main office is to maintain the order of the cosmos. The duality of the divinity

Varuna-Mitra makes Mitra the benevolent aspect of the god: Mitra watches over the moral behavior of mankind, being the tutelary deity of commitments that regulate the life of men, within family and society. Thus, the function of the cult of Mitra was to reinforce the familiar and social cohesion that structure society.

In archaic Iran, a hymn to Mithra is present in the Yašt, the Persian Old Avesta, in which the god is honored as the deity of pacts, of the day-light, and of the soldiers. With the beginning of the preaching of Zoroaster and the subsequent establishment of his religious view, the preeminent deity became Ahura Mazda‾h, who is the light who brings good. The name of Mithra vanishes from the Gatha (the literary work with Zoroaster's religious teachings) but only because the god begins to be associated with Ahura Mazda‾h itself, in accordance with the syncretic instances which witness the more ancient religious features combined with the newer ones. This discourse is valid for the post-Zoroaster period as well as the period of the conquest of Persia by Alexander the Great. With the disintegration of the Achaemenid Empire, and later on the Macedonian one after the death of Alexander, the cult of Mithra survived only in parts of Anatolia and Armenia: here Mithra still was the god of oaths, but he was progressively associated with akin Greek solar deities, specifically Apollo and Helios, with whom Mithra ended up be indiscernible from. The syncretic process that has invested Mithras makes it very difficult, if not impossible, to trace a line of continuity between the "original" Indo-European Mitra and the one of the Roman world. Considering the historical background of the cult, we see that the cult of Mithras, during the Roman Empire, is the result of a process that combines elements derived from different cultural settings: the Indo-Iranian root met with the philosophical and religious instances of Hellenic culture, and this mix has been re-elaborated to create a "new" Mithraism as a unique cult within the boundaries of the Roman Empire, characterized by specific features and relations with it.

Within the territory of the Empire, the earliest mention of the cult of Mithras is to be found in the provinces: an inscription from Nida, in the province of Germania Superior, tells us that a centurion of the cohors XXXII voluntariorum civium Romanorum made a dedication to the god. The inscription is to be dated before about 90 C.E., and it shows us that since its beginning the cult of Mithras had found support and devotees between the ranks of the army. In another inscription from Carnuntum, in the province of Pannonia, a centurion of the cohors XV legio Apollinaris consecrated an altar to Mithras. Thus, the mysteries reached quite soon both the Rhine and the Danube regions following soldiers recruited from Italy.

For what concerns Italy, the earliest inscription dedicated to Mithras is from Rome and it is part of a sculpture of the god slaying the bull: the evidence is datable to Trajan's reign (98 C.E - 117 C.E) because the inscription had been commissioned by a man named Alcimus who was the slave-administrator of Ti. Claudius Livianus, the praetorian prefect under Trajan. This dedication is important because it reveals that people from the servile class participated in the mysteries as well. The fact that the cult became important among the soldiers and the imperial administration shows that the cult of Mithras was tolerated by the authorities: although it never rose to the status of State's religion, it was quite certainly a religio licita, that means a religious congregation approved by the Empire. The reason why Mithraism came to have this status is linked to the socio-political relevance of the cult.

Mithras was the god of the contract and loyalty, and the ethic at the core of the cult is congenial to the political order: it creates a social situation dominated by a sense of cohesion and by loyalty, feelings that affected the relations of mithraists with one another as well as the one between them and the figure of the emperor. As a matter of fact, Mithraism was based on the same principles of the wider society: respect for authority, discipline and moral righteousness. It can't be a coincidence that the cult was practiced within the army, the imperial administration and the private households, all being organizations in which submission to authority is an essential element for their functioning.

The values promoted by Mithraism mirror the ones of Imperial society, creating a parallelism between the religious congregation and the strategies to maintain control in larger-scale organizations. It is quite easy to understand the role of obedience and loyalty within the army, being the conditiones sine qua non it would be impossible for it to fulfill its double function of conquest and protection of the territories of the Empire; moreover, the respect of the social hierarchy within the army and the subsequent obedience to the superiors in command were the elements used to gain promotion.

For what concern the other large-scale organization of the Roman Empire, that is the Imperial administration, it is possible to delineate a similar value-system based on obedience and diligence as the ethical conditions necessary to achieve a better position within the administrative machine; but this value-system was, simultaneously, a way to ensure a measure of control. A similar discourse can be made for the smaller organizations of private households: slaves, especially gladiators, had to be controlled because they could become a real threat to their masters.

The value-system we have been referring to, sets, as the primary virtue, obedience, which in the cult of Mithras takes the form of obedience both to the god and to the hierarchy within the cult: scholars agree in recognizing seven grades of initiation in the mysteries, from the first step that every novice must undergo, the corax, until the last one, the pater, going through the grade of the miles, the soldier. Arguably, such partition has to be linked with an astrological set of knowledge, but it also resembles a division, in terms of authority and prerogatives, that we can find in the army. The warlike attitude could be also detected in the central myth of Mithraism, that is the tauromachy: we witness Mithras riding the white bull in an attempt to overpower him, but the bull runs away and hides in a cave; later on, Mithras finds the bull and, after another fight, the god manages to kill it. The slaying of the bull is the necessary sacrifice to create life: Mithras is a demiurgic deity whose act of creation is a consequence of his victory, and the cosmological organization thus created represented a way for the devotees to find new order in a world in constant change.

Traditionally, people turn to mysteries religions when traditional frameworks and institutional authorities are in decline or failing in their mission, and this is the reason why oriental cults became popular in the Roman world during its Imperial Age.

But religion also provides a set of moral values that guides individuals to behave in accordance with a particular set of social norms: this is why, for example, we can see a revival of Mithraism's fortune after the political crisis of the III century C.E., when the Empire lived a period of military anarchy, thanks to the dedications to Mithras made by the Tetrarchs who addressed the god as protector of the empire.

Hence, Mithraism was part of Roman culture, and as such played a role as a mediator of Roman values. This is true particularly for the northern provinces, where the local élites had tight connections with the army. However, it is important to underline that Rome in its process of expansion didn't impose its religious beliefs upon the conquered territories; instead, the Roman world was characterized by tolerance and religious pluralism. In this sense, the process of integration of new populations was usually syncretic in its cultural elements.

And the god Mithras seems very well-suited to be a point of reference in a multi-ethnic and multi-cultural milieu thanks to his syncretic instances, specifically Mithras's affinity to other solar deities. Votive inscriptions and images of Mithras present the compresence, and in some cases complete identification, between him and gods such as Helios/Sol, Apollo, Serapis, as well as native solar divinities from different provinces of the Empire.

What is interesting is that in all his versions, Mithras always kept the epithet of invictus, aimed to symbolize the god's prerogatives of being the unconquerable bringer of light and life. And Mithras shared this powerful title with the god at the core of the civil religion of the Imperial Age, Sol Invictus, who was a symbol of power, eternity, and victory associated by the imperial ideology to the emperor so much that, from the Severan dynasty (193-235 C.E.), the Emperor himself began to be titled Invictus. However, there is an important difference between the cult of Mithras and the one of Sol Invictus: the latter was official. Nonetheless, the similarities in terms of symbolic representation and political relevance of the two cults – in being a tool of social control thanks to the construction of an ethic that promotes a sense of loyalty towards the Empire – explain why the cult of Mithras was not just tolerated, but often privileged by the Roman State, if compared to other "oriental" mysteries cults.

Mithraism never became an official religion, but the power of Mithraism in being accepted by different populations lies in its "global" essence, one which combines the new with the old: Mithras was a god whose existence had been enriched by elements taken from Hellenistic and oriental mysteries, as well as astrological and philosophical knowledge, in the long road that led him to Rome from Persia; this process created a deity that was able to survive for almost four centuries but that, like other pagan gods, had failed to face the coming to power of Christianity.

A MUSE BY ANY OTHER NAME

BY WAYNE GARRETH C.

I believe it was Alan Menken who described the image of the Muses in the hit Disney Animated Film Hercules to be "A Girl Group with a Whole Lotta' Gospel".

As an avid Disney fan myself, having the privilege to grow up in the Renaissance Era of Disney movies and cartoons, I marvelled over the 1997 classic Hercules for a plethora of reasons. Nevertheless, it was clear from the very opening chorus of the film that The Muses, the breakout storytellers of the marvel movie, stole the entire show with that monologue alone.

While they were vivacious, daring and extravagant in the legendary comedy, it led me to wonder, who are the Muses according to Grecian history ? Were they as astonishing in history as the blockbuster creators crafted them to be ? The path I took sought to discover just that.

The original depiction of the muses was foretold by multiple theologians, each taking on their respective interpretation. However, the most known was that by Hesiod in his Theogony (poem), regarding the muses as the nine daughters of Zeus, God of the Sky, and Mnemosyne, the Titaness of Memory. Possessing the ability to undergo metamorphosis, Zeus transformed himself into a shepherd and laid with Mnemosyne for nine nights in a row, consecrating each of the muses birthed following their consort.

It was propelled that the nine muses were the embodiment of inspiration for those gifted with creativity. Hesiod himself credited the nine muses in a hymn of dedication, opening the lines of his poem. It was his claim that the muses spoke to him on Mount Helicon, extending a laurel branch while breathing their divine voices into him, gifting him with the deific talent to profess the glory of the Grecian Gods. As it existed, art was not transferable on mediums to be immortalised by their creators. Artists of the 1st Century and beyond relied on nothing else but their memory and remembrance to spread their art throughout the world. Hesoid depicted the Muses as possessing the grace of forgetfulness; that is, forgetfulness of sorrow and overwhelming commitment. Their embodiment was purely to invigorate the vitality of Grecian art, science and literature.

Each of the nine muses acted as inspiration for a varied domain of art, science or literature, inspiring the various municipalities within Ancient Greece. While their birth order has been disputed on many occasions, the stature and inspiration each muse historically provides to whomever that worships them does not go untold. Let's take a look at each muse respectively:

Calliope

The superior muse of the nine is referred to as Calliope, and is attributed with the inspiration of epic poetry, being lengthy poems of extraordinary occurrences relating to humans in their encounters with Grecian Gods or supernatural forces. Her name bears the meaning of "the one with the beautiful voice", therefore lending an accurate depiction in the animated blockbuster as an impressive vocalist. Presiding over fluency which comes in the territory of epic poetry, the ecstatic harmony of her voice led her to inspire and chair those who sought to produce such poetry. Hesoid depicts Calliope as the wisest of all the muses, being the most decisive and confident of the nine to act as their Chief.

Calliope was believed to be the muse of Homer in the creation of his two greatest works known to man today, Iliad and Odyssey. Furthermore, she is referenced in the Divine Comedy by Dante Alighieri, worshiped in aid of his creation of Purgatorio. Modern day depictions of Calliope see her in Bob Dylan's 2020 hit song, referred to as the "Mother of the Muses". Acting as the muse to the most notorious works in education, history and literature today, Calliope's dominance in the world at large is as accomplished as her epithet suggests.

Clio

The second born muse of Zeus and Mnemosyne, Clio, would arguably resemble her mother the most. Residing effectively as the Muse of History, Clio's inspiration served as a stark reminder to those in Ancient Greece that the stories of time should never be disregarded, and the factual circumstances of events need to be reiterated to prevent the destruction of civilisation as we know it. While philosopher George Santayana may have professed the quote, "Those who do not learn history are doomed to repeat it", one may boldly suggest that his notorious statement was mused by the Goddess of History in itself.

Depicted as carrying around a book with her wherever she went, Clio's name originated from the word klieo, meaning to recount, or to remember. As some would refer to her as The Proclaimer, Clio's mark on the world can be seen in the indoctrination of Cliometrics, a varied form of economic studies, and Cliodynamics, a study of research that integrates into multiple other areas of economics and history, as core academic terms used in the University of Pennsylvania. Immortalised in a sculpture by American artist Carlo Franzoni in the National Statuary Hall at the United States Capitol, Clio's magnificence and ingenuity succours the development of latter-day historical culture.

Melpomene

While the third daughter of Zeus and Mnemosyne was named in reference to the Grecian word melpomai, meaning to celebrate song and dance, Melpomene's association with the art and creativity of ancient Greece was anything but a typical celebration. Traditionally depicted as carrying a knife accompanied by a mask bearing a face of despair with her wherever she went, Melpomene's ambition surrounded inspiring those who sought to create works of anguish, as the Goddess of Tragedy. Closely connected with her younger sister, Thalia (as discussed below), Melpomene provides the contradiction of sweet despair to the world of theatre as a balance to Thalia's bright and comedic virtue. As the goddess of tragedy, Melpomene is believed to guide the artist in their creation of distressful and sombre expression.

Eventually believed to have mothered the mermaid-like figures we now term as Sirens, Melpomene's contribution to the world of art is unlike her depiction in the 1997 animated blockbuster. Her children acted as the handmaids to the daughter of her father Zeus, and Goddess of Harvest and Fertility, Demeter, named Persephone. The inevitable abduction of Persephone by God of the Underworld, Hades, led to Demeter cursing the Sirens for all eternity, living in despair for their failure to protect Persephone. Though individually sombre and melancholy, the Grecian theatre would not be known for its excellence today without the contributions of Melpomene as a mentor for all those who create works of tragedy.

Erato

Certain obscurities when referencing the nine muses are sometimes as a result of the desire of the artists within Greece to manifest their art to a celestial status. Despite this, it was opined that there was no delusion to the muse Erato, who was described in an Orphic hymn in celebration of all the nine muses as the striking beauty on sight. Literally named the word desire in Grecian, Erato was the Goddess of Erotic Poetry and Mimic Imitation, inspiring the creation of the most salacious and titillating of art.

Her myth carries forward in the love story of Rhadine and Leonthicus, the star-crossed lovers of Samus who were murdered for their forbidden love. Their tomb, located on the island of Samus, was recognised as the pilgrim site for star-crossed lovers during the period of the 100 AD. Erato's close relationship with Eros, known poignantly with his well-known name, Cupid, lends itself to her depiction as a wanderer with golden arrows, seeking out any hopeless romantic to strike. Her numerous mentions in philosophical extracts, including Hesoid's Theogony, Plato's Phaedrus and Virgil's Aenid leave no grey areas as to the insurmountable desire Grecian mortals had for her presence.

Euterpe

The fifth daughter of Zeus and Mnemosyne had her influence in the art of song and music, recognised as the Muse of Lyrical Poetry to be exact. Referred to as the "Giver of Delight", Euterpe is often depicted with a double flute, also known as an aulos. Beyond that, others have also accounted her as being the creator of multiple wind instruments, contributing directly to those who sought to create musical works of wonder by invoking her name. Exercising her inspiration towards divine lyricists and poets, Euterpe is highly regarded as the reason of progress for the field of liberal and fine art. Her stimulus extends to encompass the creativity of individuals in numerous areas of art, uniting them by lyric and rhythm.

Notwithstanding her musical talents, Euterpe's presence is not described in detail beyond her birthing Rhesus, the Thracian king who fought in the Trojan war. Nevertheless, her contributions and notoriety in popular culture is depicted by her engraving on a Roman mint of Quintus Pomponius Musa, a moneyer who commissioned the design of royal mints in references to famous mythological and historical beings. While each muse was depicted in a singular design, the most commonly referenced and favoured to is that of Euterpe.

Terpsichore

The Muse of Dance and Chorus is known by the name of Terpsichore. As the sixth daughter of Zeus and Mnemosyne, her name was derived from the Grecian adjective terpsichorean, which directly relates to instances of dance or relating to dance. The animated classic depicted the goddess as a breath of fresh air, moving to the beat of any song while also staying true to herself at every step. Just as her sisters however, Terpsichore was described as radiant and talented, carrying a harp as her symbol of notability, though she was gifted in many other instruments as well.

It was conceivable that her gifts were dazzled by many artists who accredit her to their works, including that by the collector Michael Praetorius, singer Frank Sinatra, and the production of an entire series surrounding the Goddess of Dance in the cult television classic, Xena: Warrior Princess. French dancer Marie-Madeleine Guimard went on to name a private theatre in her palace the Temple of Terpsichore in 1766, envisioning the space as inspiration from the muse herself. Though the palace has since been demolished, it was most known for the Temple of Terpsichore within it, enlightened with the 500-seat hippodrome and neoclassical style architecture.

Urania

Though it may seem odd, one should not question the possibility of Grecian Gods playing favourites when it comes to their children. Noticeably or not, Zeus and Mnemosyne choosing to name their seventh daughter together, as Urania, may be a tilt of the hat to her grandfather, Uranus, the primordial Titan of whom acted as the embodiment of the sky, and father to Mnemosyne. Notably recognised as carrying a compass and globe in her hands, Urania, also known as Ouranía, is a direct translation of heavenly.

Believed to have been responsible for the evolution of liberal arts in Greece, astronomers oft invoke her guide in the name of astronomical discovery. No greater privilege did a muse bear than by having a planet named after her partially, together with her grandfather. Eventual accounts also describe Urania as being the muse of Christian poets, particularly being invoked in John Milton's poem, Paradise Lost. Power is bestowed onto the muse who may not be recognised in pop culture or the literary arts as frequently as her other sisters, but is immortalised in the world of stargazers and devotees of the Christian faith.

Thalia

It would come as no surprise that the comedic relief brought by the muse Thalia in the 1997 classic resembles her mythological counterpart in spirit. Recognised as the second youngest of the nine muses, Thalia was referred to as the goddess who presided over humour and comedy, as well as idyllic poetry, taking on the inverse inspiration to her Chief muse, Calliope, and her sister of tragedy and despair, Melpomene. A key aspect of entertainment for ancient Greeks was that of theatre performance. The legendary "Melpomene and Thalia" masks, otherwise known as the theatre masks, is a gracious nod to the Goddess of Comedy Thalia herself, while the weeping mask is in reference to her muse sister, Melpomene. Portrayed wearing a crown of ivy, Thalia is also envisioned with a trumpet and bugle, which were pronounced instruments in the theatre.

While Thalia was the muse for multiple works of Apollodorus and Diodurus, her mark on Grecian mythology differed from her sisters through her humour and relatability. Purported to be the muse that spent the most time with the human race, Thalia motivated artists and theatre performers alike to create and perform. Additionally acting as an entertainer to the deities of Olympus, Thalia's presence and light-hearted energy ensured that her stories never made it sound like some Greek tragedy.

Polyhymnia

The youngest muse has not seen much depiction in modern day art or entertainment, despite her contributions being varied and aplenty. Going by the name of Polyhymnia, "Poly" lending itself to the term many, the goddess is referred to as the inspiration for sacred hymns, pantomimes, meditation, and even that of geometry in science. Described as very serious and contemplative by nature, Italian historian Didorus accredits Polyhymnia as the guide and inspiration for many glorious authors, including Dante Alighieri and Ovid.

As her name suggests, Polyhymnia aided mortals in diverse fields of the arts and sciences. Grecian historian Diodorus Siculus claimed that Polyhymnia's great praise brought a distinct clarity to writers and fabricators, enlightening them with immortal fame. Diodorus himself went on to create the monumental Bibliotheca Historica, known as one of the colossal contributions to universal history to date. In 1854, French astronomer Jean Chacornac named his discovery of an asteroid belt after the goddess, "33 Polyhymnia", enshrining the muse eternally. Lesser-known to her counterparts and sisters, it is undoubted that Polyhymnia's contributions to the array fields of art and science make her one of the most diverse Goddesses in Grecian history.

(From left to right: Calliope, Euterpe, Thalia, Melpomene, Terpsichore, Erato, Clio, Urania, Polyhymnia).

The 'Muse' is not an artistic mystery, but a mathematical equation. The gift are those ideas you think of as you drift to sleep. The giver is that one you think of when you first awake. Author Roman Payne was certain that a muse is not one who is unbeknownst to the creator of a work of art, but instead a factor of the subconscious when their minds are dedicated only to the progress and prosperity of a chosen discipline.

The phenomenon of the muses as symbols of innovation and expression to the ancient artists of Greece was accepted not only in worship, but the concoction of an entire indoctrination dedicated to the muses. Several shrines and temples have been consecrated in dedication to the muses. The two most notable locations of worship being Mount Helicon in Boiotia, where Zeus and Mnemosyne conceived the muses, and Peria, located in Macedonia.

Mathematician Pythagoras advised the people of Croton to construct a shrine to the muses to stand in the centre of the city, promoting the civic of learning and harmony amongst one another. It was claimed by the philosopher Cicero in his book De Natura Deorum that Pythagoras would sacrifice an ox in dedication to the Muses when he devised novel geometrical works and study. I anticipate no reader would earnestly act on the suggestion of sacrificing an ox for their art, but the crux of the imprint the muses have left with individuals is without a doubt, one of the greatest influences not only in theology and philosophy, but in modern culture and entertainment in the present day as well.

The next time you are looking for a slice of inspiration, take some time out to give reverence to a muse of your choice, or all if you need more assistance. The greatness of the Goddesses of Art, Science and Literature shan't leave you disheartened.

Bibliography

1.Remembrance: The Nine Muses in Greek Mythology | Pinterest.

2.Which of the Nine Muses Guide You? | Winning the Business.

3.The Nine Muses of Greek Mythology | Greek Myths & Greek Mythology.

4.Muse | Brittanica.

5.Who Were The Nine Greek Muses? | Thought.Co.

6.Hercules (1997) Film | Wikipedia.

7.Muses | Greek Mythology Link.

LITERATURE

BIRTH OF A PESSIMIST

BY ABRAHAM ADZASHOJA

The Conception

How are men born? Are they hatched in eggs or are they bred in water? How convenient would it be if men were nested on trees and nurtured by wild fruits—then everyone would be a mother.

Child birth has been described as one of the most excruciating pains a woman experience. Women go through undulating levels of labour just to bring a child into the world. But when that child is born, the pain goes away. Pain it seems, stays only long enough to deliver an outcome. Thus, we can agree it is pain that births. While the pain of a mother produces a bundle of joy, pain doesn't always bring much pleasurable things. Pain can either produce an outcome, or it could be the effect of an outcome—something we wish shouldn't have happened at all.

Pessimism is conceived in wombs of experience and nourished in shells of broken spirits—birthing emotions muffled in swaddles of gloom. When the mind has been yielded as breeding ground for despair, the fecundation of dejection will spread to other areas of the victim's life, battering them in the process. Pain shoots like sticky arrows that pierce the heart of its victim— belabouring them over and over again, till they're left lying in puddles of their own blood; blood they cannot see. We bleed more internally than we do externally.

Pessimists are not solely born of women; they're also born of moments. Moments that hang in isolation, like placards of all that went wrong. Pessimists are people lost in moments, trying to cage what once was, and imagining what could be had tragedy not struck. It's so easy to write them off as nugatory elements of the society. But if we are not so cruel as to conclude they are insane; we'll see that they once believed in something. Once upon a time they were believers, who held on to a cause, an ideology or philosophy that helped shape their world. Tragedy however, became the habitat for the birthing of new things in them they wished never saw the light of day.

The death of one thing, is the birth of another. Truth be told, every one of us has at one point or the other harboured pessimism. We've all had unforgiving moments that tenaciously swayed our focus from the bigger picture. Our saving grace; we were able to wriggle out of it before many eyes feasted on us.

Grief when unbridled, deteriorates; whether visible or not, until it forms a cascade of murky emotions which go on rampage, further impairing one's outlook on life. The end result is a defeated fellow who doesn't believe the future holds anything of worth.

Pessimists are people who have been widowed by ideas they held to in the past. But like most widows, they simply don't have the strength to love again. But while they think they're living free of the enclave of marriage, they unconsciously become espoused to the idea of being alone. The cessation of a course, is the emergence of another.

People have varying ways of coping with pain. While some seem to get over it almost immediately, some take longer times to heal. The end result however is that each person finds a way to continue living—gainfully or not.

Once I knew a woman. She lost her sanity after witnessing the gruesome murder of her husband. Those savages snuffed out life from the very person that gave her a reason to live. For her, the murderers killed two persons that day. It was the end of her world as she knew it. She left home and found an abode along the street of a busy town. She was in plain sight, but few ever saw her— perfectly hidden under the eyes of the world around. Her children usually brought her food in expensive flasks; but I doubt she ever ate from there.

Many would see her as a mad woman, but I see her as one betrayed by the State—thus, she has the full right to become a renegade; that's if she still had control of her mind. A man is not insane, to whom life was sane.

When the State fails to provide such basic things as protection, job and job security, and all of these basic human needs—it opens up myriads of other possibilities. Even the most loyal and patriotic person is left jostling options withing his mind on how best to survive.

The betrayal

Consider this fellow who gets himself a gun; he only has the gun because the State failed to provide the basic need of protection for him. Perhaps he has lost a loved one at the hands of cold-blooded murderers. So, he has the gun for protection; but if this same State fails to provide a job for him, he then begins to nurse the plethora of ungodly options available to him with a gun in his possession. He sees that he can scare off a few people with it by waving it in their faces and collect their money, just to feed, he convinces himself.

He has a successful first night; turns out people are really afraid of guns. It was risky, and his conscience was bleeding, almost choking him. Words go on rampage in his mind, a brutal opposition. But he convinces himself he had no option. He thought that would be the last time he would do that.

You can't tame nature; two nights roll on and his stomach cries with grumblings so violent the person standing by could hear them. He has no one to turn to, so he goes out again, hoping like before, this would be the last time. Turns out he lied, as he's gone back now for more rounds than he can count. This fellow is getting lost, and he can feel it—but he feels helpless. After a while, his little secret leaks out, and word spreads fast. He's now an official armed robber. The State comes after him, intending to make a show of him to the public. To them, he has become the opposite of all the State preaches—officially, he's branded a **renegade**.

My proposition is that there are renegades who were first betrayed by the State. A child that is left alone in a forest should not be blamed if he behaves more animal-like than human. We become what surrounds us; or dare I say, we become what we surround ourselves with.

Renegades throw questions at us they aren't really asking. We hear them shout questions at us without ever opening their mouths. We must realise in such moments that it's our hearts that judge us. For if we see some of these misled ones and we don't take pity on them as victims of a failed system, then, our humanity is in question. In the same vein, if we see them consumed by vices and we only gaze on or cheer, then we push them further into their own destruction. While the humane thing to do is to see renegades as humans, equal as we are, we are not to justify the course they have taken.

The cutlass that broke the coconut also brought out the juice in it; one cause—two effects. The famous story in the holy book then comes to mind of how Moses, struck the red sea with his rod, the water parted and the Israelites walked over on dry ground. Isn't it ironic then that this same water which parted for one people, became the grave of another—as the Egyptians drowned trying to cross it. People have gone through similar things but came out differently.

What constitutes betrayal may be one's way of rendering retribution to the State that failed him. You see, it is not only the State that can punish. When what could have been avoided happens, outrage becomes the normal reaction from the victims.

How do you explain a situation where a student goes to school obviously for the purpose of learning in order to become a useful member of the society—but while he is there, lecturers make it their daily routine to insult, demean and frustrate him. As he is enduring this to just finish his studies and leave all that behind, he gets kidnapped by people he has neither met in his life nor offended directly. He's kept in captivity, amidst several unheeded pleas by the poor parents. His gay captors sexually molest him, every single day.

Days grow into weeks, and weeks become months and there's still no sign of rescue. Rays of hope grow dim, and the sun of despondency sets on him. The demise of the last glimmer of optimism this person had, was also the elimination of every strand of faith they still had in the State. Another pessimist has just been born.

The proliferation of renegades can be controlled. What would be our fate if we all wake up one day and find more people infested with melancholia than those who may not be so contented, but still believe that things will become better? We can act now before the sun sets on us.

THE MODERN WORLD

BY ROCÍO DIKÚN

The last decades of the nineteenth century, as well as the early years of the twentieth century, were accompanied by a great deal of global developments. The advancement of technology culminated in life-changing achievements in matter of hard sciences alongside social sciences. As a result, between 1880 and 1917 writers reveal themselves against the order established beforehand, and give rise to a completely different way of not only writing, but also experiencing the world and life itself. This new perception derived into the so know movement called "Modernism."

Modernist literature considers reality and the human nature to have intrinsically changed, and a discontinuity between the conservative past and the promising future to have occurred. From that point onward, the world would never be as it had been before. Society made a drastic alteration never experienced by humanity, and issues of common interest began acquiring a place on the spotlight.

Concerns involving social studies and humanities gave rise to an array of new ideas that led to the establishment of various priorities. One of those priorities was the management of the concept of the human mind; it went from being an accessory addition to the human body that allowed individuals to think and function, to being the essential tool that made people who they are. Accordingly, when it became extremely noticeable that the mind was as important as the body, the study of the conscious and the unconscious came to the forefront and shed light to revolutionary statements that would change the world forever.

Highly influenced by the development of psychology and the studies of the unconscious mind, writers discovered a tool to express their avant-grade attitudes towards the traditional concepts and ideas employed up to that time. Hence, in the process of that pursue, they attained the creation of stories like no others. Said stories allow the reader to deepen the relationship with the characters by getting inside their heads and feeling the heroes' feelings. Stories went from being plot and action driven to being character driven.

A new perspective on the world and human existence leads to radical innovations in style and language. In modern stories, outer reality becomes secondary and human consciousness comes to the fore, while creating several different scenarios, situations and dilemmas. With every second that goes by, the mind increasingly creates new worlds out its own viewpoints and considerations. The absence of plot and action prevails and the writer focuses on the inner conflicts of the hero in such a way that the reader becomes blind to objective reality. The reader can only experience the world through the main character's eyes and perception. It is unknown whether the hero tells the truth or not as it is heavily charged with subjectivity. Modern writers appeal to this resource to express the real nature of human queries feasibly, insomuch as the lack of plot and the emphasis on human consciousness prevents the reader from understanding the world beyond the main character's feelings and thoughts. In terms of grammar modifications, in an attempt to resemble the flow of human thoughts, writers showcase very few pauses and punctuation marks all through their stories.

The new found significance of human consciousness resulted in the development of the nowadays renowned stream of consciousness technique. This style of writing, adopted by all modern writers, sought to place the attention on the character's inner conflicts and internal world as opposed to external sources of information. What is more, the mind acquires the role of enemy against human beings to such an extent that during the internal monologue the reader experiences there is a total display of the main character's traumas, disturbances and insecurities as well as their incapability to solve them. The self metamorphoses into the centre and driving force of the whole story and seeks to associate its preoccupations with superior values. Correspondingly, for the first time in the history of literature, the reader comes across characters that possess the virtues of the hero and the antagonist within themselves.

It should be noted that, whereas the past was centred on searching answers, modernism is concerned about creating unanswered questions and displaying the fight of the hero against its own demons. The hero is its own worst enemy and their problems always remain unresolved. As a result, human beings define themselves and their authenticity by the queries they allow to anguish them. Owing to the fact that modernism thrives on metaphysical predicaments, characters question themselves and the meaning of life simultaneously. Therefore, as they become sincere with themselves regarding their feelings, they learn to find comfort in their sadness and emotional wounds.

It goes without saying that, with the rise of a totally new manner of writing and experiencing reality, the modern hero embodies characteristics never witnessed before. Modernism stepped away from the conception of heroes being "chosen ones" who are destined upon birth to save the world; and created characters that do not believe themselves to possess the qualities necessary in order to make an impact on the society they find themselves immersed in.

The main character is aware of the fact that society and humanity needs and must change but they feel unfit to carry out such duty. Accordingly, they see the world beyond them as a reflection of what they experience within themselves. Due to the intensity of their feelings, instead of focusing on the actions they consider should be undertaken for the sake of modifying society's flaws, they become trapped in their own unconscious to such an extent that they end up being paralysed by their own fears.

The bravery or capability of the modern hero is never in question; however, it is their own psychological trauma that which prevents them from achieving their purpose. As a matter of fact, the modern hero embarks on their odyssey expecting to transform the world but nonetheless, when facing inconveniences, the query "Can I change myself?" arises. When standing before this question, the hero experiences a psychic battlefield where feelings such as insecurity, inadequacy and unworthiness make themselves present; and situations that appear to be extremely uncomplicated become charged with subjectivity.

Mabel, the main character of Virginia Woolf's masterpiece "The New Dress" embodies all the characteristics the modern hero is said to incarnate. Mabel is a mother and a wife who has lived in the shadow ever since she could remember. Due to this, she resolves to make an appearance at Mrs. Dalloway's party wearing an extremely flamboyant yellow dress. She decides to carry out an action such unlike her out of desire of being original and drawing positive attention. She dreamed of the moment when aristocrats and individuals belonging to the upper class would compliment her appearance, endorse her presence and accept her as one of their own. However, as soon as she arrives to the party, feelings of inadequacy, self-consciousness and inferiority overpower her. From the moment she decided to attend the party her desires and objectives were extremely clear in her mind; nevertheless, when facing the actual situation, she finds herself lacking the character and psychological strength to fulfil her aspirations.

Mabel becomes tremendously weary with all the detrimental thoughts going through her mind, and turns increasingly aware of the discrepancies between the people in the party and herself. Neither does she belong to the upper class nor does she blend in with the crowd due to her new dress. Thereby, her initial plans of standing out thanks to her beauty and uniqueness turn against her and the last thing she wants is to be noticed. Accordingly, her yellow dress represents the manifestation of all her inner conflicts, as it is the tangible object she can hold onto to account for her feelings and unresolved traumas.

In spite of being well educated, Mabel suffers from an appalling inferiority complex that does not allow her to feel entitled to be the source of change in such a closed off society. This is highly noticeable in the fact that "She saw herself like that — she was a fly, but the others were dragonflies, butterflies, beautiful insects, dancing, fluttering, skimming, while she alone dragged herself up out of the saucer." Whereas she considers individuals around her to represent beautiful, colourful, graceful insects, she thinks herself to be a fly, so trapped in her own mind that she fails to perceive all her qualities and potential. She despises herself to the extent of using dreadful adjectives such as coward, envious, spiteful and vain to describe herself.

Over and above, it should be noted that, as distinctive of modern heroes when facing an unchangeable reality, Mabel envisions an alternative life where she can be exactly like everyone else. The fact that she desires to make such a change in her personality displays that she does not wish to pretend to be someone she is not anymore. This longing is revealed when her thoughts establish: "She would wear a uniform; she would be called Sister Somebody" meaning that she craves the moment she gets to leave to a place where she could help others while being unseen and unnoticed. As a matter of fact, the uniform itself exhibits an extreme lack of individuality, as it creates the collective illusion of several people being and looking alike.

By the end of the story, Mabel is aware of the fact that, if she had been confident and bold enough to continue the pursuit she arrived looking for, she would have been able to achieve her goal of being acknowledged and seen for her originality and authenticity. However, the "water in her veins", that is to say her lack of strength in character, prevents her from accomplishing the heroes' journey. She even reaches the point of pretending nothing has happened and she is perfectly fine by stating that "she has enjoyed herself enormously" before the hostess. In doing so, Mabel succumbs to her own insecurities and fears and decides to embrace her social mask once and for all.

In conclusion, modernism was an experiment in literature that derived from the development of psychology and became the signature of some of the most famous writers all over the world. This literary movement gave the reader an active role in the story and allowed them to create a completely different bond with the characters that had never been experienced before. It resulted in character driven stories where individuals, not only fall in love with images created in their minds with the assistance of beautiful words; but also understand and relate to the hero on a deeper level. It made individuals feel closer as a society and encouraged acceptance and human connections through emotions, understanding and empathy.

ART HISTORY

THE BIRTH OF A WORLD

BY MOHAMMAD ABEDI

The Renaissance can not be described as just an artistic movement, but the Renaissance was a great cultural, scientific and artistic event that took place between the fourteenth and seventeenth centuries. This movement influenced all the social currents of Europe at that time, and in other words, through it, the Western world entered the period of modernity from the Middle Ages. This movement was the beginning of great artistic, cultural and scientific leaps. And many philosophical, social, and sociological concepts today are rooted in this movement. The word renaissance means rebirth. The word is derived from the Italian word Rinascimento and from the Italian verb nascere meaning birth. But the foundation of the Renaissance school is based on Humanism. The concept itself is derived from the teachings of classical Rome, and classical Roman civilization owes this concept to ancient Greece. In general, the theory of humanism is derived from the theory of the ancient Greek sophist philosopher Protagoras. His famous statement that man is the center of everything is very important in this school.

The image you see is Vitruvian Man. This work is one of the most important and prominent symbols of the Renaissance and the proportions of the human body, which is also one of the symbols of humanism. This famous work belongs to the genius of all times Leonardo da Vinci

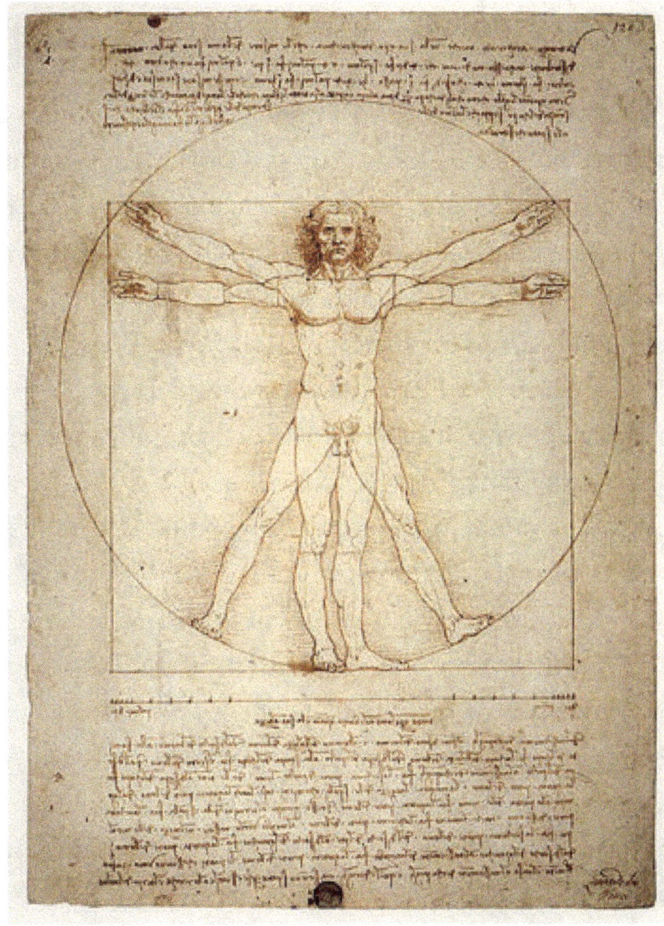

The Italian artist and art critic Giorgio Vasari first used the term Renaissance in 1550 in Lives of the Most Excellent Painters, Sculptors, and Architects.

In this book he wrote a text about the Gothic style. Part of this text is as follows: The glorious art declined and perished with the collapse of the Roman Empire. Only Tuscan art has been the savior of art in Europe. Artists such as Giotto and Cimabue have done the job. Note that Gothic art was not considered valuable by Vasari, and he considered real art to be the classical teachings of ancient Rome and Greece. After mentioning this word in the book of Vazari, this phrase remained almost useless until the nineteenth century AD, and it was in the nineteenth century that the word Renaissance was used in France.

The word was first used in France by the French critic and historian Jules Michel, and has since gained worldwide fame. But as mentioned, the root of this word is completely Italian and basically the birthplace and origin of this movement is Italy. In his book, Jules Michele referred to the Renaissance as a scientific, cultural, and artistic movement that had previously been considered much more limited and detailed.

But a famous Swiss historian, Carl Jacob Burckhardt, in his book published in 1860, also introduces the Renaissance from the fourteenth to the sixteenth century. He described the Renaissance as inspiring the spirit of individualism and humanism in the future. His book was very well received.

The Renaissance movement as a whole led to the birth of a new way of thinking that had a profound effect on architecture, politics, science, and literature. One of the initial effects and results of this great movement is the invention of concrete and the invention of perspective, both of which had many effects on architecture and painting.

On the other hand, the invention of lead printing caused the spread of scientific sources in the form of books throughout Europe, and this caused the awareness of various sections of society. But the Renaissance, in its very early stages, showed signs of its emergence in Italy and the late thirteenth century with Dante's writings and Giotto's paintings. The Renaissance, as a cultural movement, gained strength in the early fourteenth century with the flourishing of Latin literature.

This continued with the re-reading of classical sources and literature. One of the leaders was the Italian poet, historian, writer and anthropologist Francesco Petrarch. He is known as the father of the school of humanism, and he was greatly inspired by a great poet and writer like Shakespeare.

The origin and starting point of this movement in Italy can be Florence.

For many historians, the question arises as to why this movement began in a small town like Florence. One reason is the Medici family.

The powerful Duke of Florence, Lorenzo Medici, has always been a supporter of the region's artists. He has always been an inspiration to important Florentine artists such as Leonardo da Vinci, Sandro Botticelli and Michelangelo. The three great artists were also born in the province of Tuscany, centered in Florence

But this massive movement gradually spread beyond the borders of Italy. In England, the Renaissance began around the 16th century. And one of the famous and great figures of this period is William Shakespeare. In fact, the Renaissance movement in England was very different from the Italian one. In England, the movement was based more on literature and music, and the visual arts in that country were very limited at that time. In general, this artistic movement in England began very late (around 1520 AD).

In the year 1495 AD, the Renaissance came to France. Naturally, this artistic movement came to France through Italy. The Renaissance came to France by King Charles VIII after his invasion of Italy. After Charles VIII, Francis I began to further the Renaissance in France. He began to build palaces and buildings in the Renaissance style. One of the most important French painters of that time was Jean-Claude, who also painted a portrait of Francis I. Despite all this, the art of painting in France at that time was still relatively far from the Italian type in terms of technique.

In northern Europe, this artistic movement became known as the Northern Renaissance. Like England, Italian Renaissance painting was quite different from the Northern Renaissance. Italian painters were among the first painters to paint scenes with non-religious themes. These artists violated the rules and regulations of medieval art and dealt with new themes and subjects in the visual arts. In contrast, Northern Renaissance artists initially remained faithful to and worked on religious themes and themes. If we want to cite a very important and obvious example of Northern European artists, we can mention the great painter Albrecht Dürer.

Perspective was one of the most important factors in the growth of realist painting during the Renaissance, and on the other hand, the study of the great artists of that time on light, shadow and colors led to a stunning leap in painting. In addition, the studies and works of the great genius Leonardo da Vinci in human anatomy led to great advances in the art of figurative painting. The works of these artists, in addition to the works of Raphael, led to the creation of a special artistic style, so that other artists began to study the works of these three great artists (Raphael, Leonardo and Michelangelo) and other beautiful works emerged from these studies. If we want to name other remarkable and great artists of this period, we can mention Donatello in Florence and Thyssen in Venice. One of the greatest masterpieces of the Renaissance is the painting of The School of Athens by Raphael. In this beautiful work of art, the faces of many famous Greek philosophers can be seen. This work is considered as one of the greatest masterpieces of the Renaissance and has a classical spirit.

During the Renaissance, perspective became fully scientific and the consequence of the invention of scientific perspective was the birth of the Camera Obscura. In fact, the idea and concept of the camera was invented and discovered during the Renaissance, and then completed and became what it is today. This technique was first used by great painters to better achieve the proper composition and proportions of the human figure. The Camera Obscura thus became a tool for use in drawing and painting.

In the end, it should be said that the Renaissance was a huge multifaceted movement that really affected the whole future and human life on the planet. Many of the inventions and births of artists and scientists after the Renaissance are indeed due to this scientific, cultural, artistic and social movement. Many of the events that lie ahead, such as the Industrial Revolution and the avant-garde art movement, are indeed rooted in the great Renaissance movement.

OTHER ARTICLES

BLADE RUNNER AND POSTMODERNISM

BY OLIVIA SIMONE

Blade Runner (1982) is a science fiction film directed by Ridley Scott, inspired by Philip K. Dick's novel Do Androids Dream of Electric Sheep? (1968). The film depicts Rick Deckard, a "blade runner", as he attempts to hunt down four synthetic humans—bioengineered by Tyrell Corporation—who have escaped their positions at the space colonies and illegally returned to Earth. This essay discusses how Blade Runner can be interpreted as a postmodern text, through the manipulation of narrative and mise-en-scene and Scott's subsequent alterations that led to the 2007 final cut.

As a movement, Postmodernism was founded on scepticism and established a suspicion of reason. Throughout Blade Runner, the narrative confronts our grounded distinction between real and counterfeit. Upon meeting, Deckard asks Rachael if the owl is artificial, to which she replies, 'of course it is' (Blade Runner: 2007). By contrast, Rachael is unaware that she is a replicant, as captured in Deckard's interrogative utterance to Tyrell, 'how can it not know what it is?' (Blade Runner: 2007). This juxtaposition between Rachael's certainty regarding the 'realness' of the animal and that of herself.

It is important to note the contrast in her certainty regarding the 'realness' of the animal, and herself; as captured in Deckard's interrogative utterance to Tyrell, 'how can it not know what it is?' (Blade Runner: 2007). This juxtaposition in Rachael's mind blurs the definition of what it means to

be synthetic and the criterion for being alive. The existence of the synthetic humans, known as replicants, proposes the question, is believing you are human adequate to be defined as human? Indeed, the manner in which this concept within the film cannot be rationalized by conformist science or thought reinforces the Postmodernist interpretation of Blade Runner. Modernism supported that reality could be recognised and understood by particular collective principles, such as those formulated by science or religion. Postmodernism as a reaction to Modernist thought rejects this assumption, which is encapsulated in the complex notions of existence that permeate throughout Blade Runner. Following Rachael's voight-kampff test, Tyrell jovially explains to Deckard that 'more human than human' is his motto (Blade Runner: 2007). Here, Tyrell's statement appears to encapsulate the epitomy of Postmodernist uncertainty that is present in the film and can be construed as a rejection of the humanist self. Replicants have the ability to reason, and thus mirror that of a 'real' human; therefore the definition of human and the concept of humanity completely collapses.

To elaborate, the overwhelming emotions experienced by Roy Batty as he approaches his imminent death emphatically frames the tentative distinction between human and electric. After Roy saves Deckard from falling to his death, he explains that 'I've seen things you people wouldn't believe [...] All those moments will be lost in time.' (Blade Runner: 2007). While the voight-kampff test utilises empathy as the distinguishing factor between human and replicant, Rutger Hauer's emotional portrayal of Roy demonstrates the closeness between real and artificial in the film. Customarily, Postmodernist art poses as an advocate for the exposition of personal experience, which is portrayed in Roy's final declaration that continues to disrupt our understanding of being human. Succeeding Roy's decease, in the 1982 adaptation, Deckard's voice over states, 'I don't know why he let me live. Maybe in those last moments he loved life more than he ever had. Not just his life [...] My life' (Blade Runner: 1982). Here, Roy's apparent appreciation for existing markedly contrasts with the reoccurring belief that empathy for life is what differentiates humans and replicants. This scene does, in fact, suggest quite the opposite—humans and replicants are essentially symmetrical, both alive and living; which does, of course, reflect how Postmodernism frequently embraces contradictory tiers of meaning.

Nonetheless, given that the defining elements of the Postmodern are somewhat ambiguous, Blade Runner can, to some extent, be viewed as a Modernist text; the conflict of old and new, a seedy depiction of a detective protagonist filled with turmoil. However, the changed narrative in the 2007 final cut realigns the film with Postmodernism. Fundamentally, the ending of Blade Runner (2007) rejects the universal truth that a 'happy ending' exists. By inserting the unicorn dream sequence the origami unicorn carries a greater significance and suggests that Deckard's dreams, and therefore his memories, are not his own so he must be a replicant. The idea of being uncertain about who you are, is echoed in Blade Runner 2049, when Joe believes he is Deckard's son. Ergo, the final cut reinforces the Postmodern status of Blade Runner as it defies reason and refuses to use societally shared truths to explain reality. Perhaps, the alteration of the ending also speaks to a shift in the hegemonic interests of popular culture. In 1982, nine years before the end of the Cold War, mass audience possibly preferred the opportunity for a happy ending, in search for a sense of escapism (Blumler and Katz: 1973). By contrast, the emergent use of a sinister, increasingly mysterious, ending was favoured by dominant culture in the 21st century. Interestingly, the manner in which Scott iteratively revisited Blade Runner highlights how, even as a creator, he experienced an aurora of scepticism surrounding his work.

In the congregation of film noir and science fiction, Blade Runner also conforms to the Postmodernist encouragement of combining divergent genres and rejecting the dominance of one particular style. Blade Runner captures the essence of film noir through the overarching mood of pessimism and fatalism present in the orientalised city; the murder of Luba Luft certainly epitomises a film noir atmosphere. Simultaneously, Scott's creation shares normative qualities with science fiction, as portrayed through the flying cars, manufacture of replicants, and overall futuristic elements in the mise-en-scene. The collision of these genres is repeatedly depicted through the use of technology—specifically, while the guns do have quasi-lasers they appear somewhat out-dated. Therefore, by merging the residual, that being aspects of film noir, with the emergent, as contemporary science fiction was, Blade Runner further presents itself as a Postmodernist text. Furthermore, Scott's production explicitly frames a collision of high and low culture. After Roy visits Tyrell and violently kisses him, the replicant gouges Tyrell's eyes into his skull. The lewd nature of this scene implicitly alludes to the story of Oedipus, which can be aligned with high culture. Nonetheless, the manner in which this quasi-Oedipal act is placed within the realm of science fiction symbolises a deconstruction in the segregation between high and low culture.

Ultimately then, to define Blade Runner as a Postmodernist text is to evaluate the concept of the Postmodern and recognise how the aesthetics of the film can be intertwined with this movement.

Bibliography

Blade Runner. 1982. [Film]. Ridley Scott. dir. USA: The Ladd Company Shaw Brothers.
Blade Runner. 2007. [Film]. Ridley Scott. dir. USA: The Ladd Company Shaw Brothers.

POETRY

IT'S ALRIGHT FOR MARCUS AURELIUS.

BY BRONWEN EVANS

And so I dwelled when I was young

Before tragedy struck in violent waves,

In the stoicism of Marcus Aurelius

Never another my sun could shade,

But then was cursed by Cassandra's tongue

And all of those who failed us blind,

Who failed you and me, who failed themselves

And cast shadow when they came to light

Upon my words, all I had heard

Until the mists were cleared by night

To realise I all along was right.

Who saw Medusa's viper nest

And called them in with sharpened swords

When I and she and her and we

Sing desperate of the mixed up chords

Of blame and men, their jealousy

Their mirrors and their enrolment forced

And how the scapegoat came to be

While the treacherous pretend to turn to stone.

The more innocent that we are sometimes

The more the bitter come for thee

Through ancient valleys lined with bones

From weak souls deceit and trickery.

THE HUMAN TOUCH

BY SOUMYA KARKERA

All it took is a global pandemic
For us to realize the value,
Of human touch
By texting that friend,
You had lost touch
In the rat race of
Making money
Adulting,
Calling our families
And talking to them
Within the screens
Of our phones,
Children glued
To their chairs
In online lectures
Instead of the
Bench desk
And blackboard,
Adults making money
In front of their laptops
By ruining their sleep, hunger,
In order to bring food to the table
And money in their bank accounts,
We are now in a time and age
Where a hug and a kiss
Is more valuable than
Millions of rupees and
All the luxuries of the world

THE THING ABOUT AN EMPTY ROOM

BY NUEL UYI

The thing about

An empty room

Is that

It has a sense

Of abandonment

And sinks into the quicksand of loneliness.

Overcome by melancholy,

The room stares into space,

Its thoughts drifting towards

Pleasant memories

Once spent

In the company of its beloved.

Those were the days!

Moments when the room brimmed

With laughter

Like an overflowing glass of wine.

Alas!

These four walls

Now echo back the voice of the room.

YOU! (NOT A NETFLIX SERIES)

BY SUDAKSHINA BHATTA

I wish I were lucky as you,

Having someone to forever love you,

A best friend and a best critic for you,

Someone, who would do anything for you,

Yet making sure, not to cause any disruptions for you,

Someone, ready to take up challenges for you,

Someone, patiently dealing with the tantrums thrown by you,

Getting hurt & wounded unknowingly by you,

That someone, still manages to overlook them, because what matters is you,

Someone ignoring the long queue behind, just for you,

Someone sticking around, when asked to leave by you,

Someone, not asking a single question, knowing those would bother you,

Someone, wondering about the health conditions of you,

Someone, sending silent "take care" for you

Someone, never expressing yet silently missing you,

Someone, knowing that once they got misled by you,

Yet that someone, not being able to completely mistrust you,

Someone, familiar with the infamous mood swings of you,

Someone, acquainted with the forgotten promises by you,

Someone, keenly observing the drastic change in you,

Someone not dumping their hopes and expectations on you,

Someone, not trying to blindly worship you,

Because that someone, prefers to see the human in you,

Someone, treasuring the pictures of you,

Someone, cherishing the moments spent with you,

Someone, finding the marshmallow built cute about you,

Someone, willing to leave their everything for you,

Someone, waiting for a change of mind in you,

Someone, accepting every flaw in you,

Someone, who isn't praying for perfection in you,

Rather, willing to walk beside the distorted, imperfect you!

THE FOG OF VELVET SKIES

BY OLIVIA SIMONE

Feeling Fog

Like a saturated grey skies borrowing within

Velvet?

Cascading between the life above

But

My mind contracted to the fog

Obliged to disquiet

I am beholden to the skies of those below and

Opposite.

Holding on to stagnation,

To a reality.

Rain trickling between my fingers

Droplets bestowing themselves upon my toes

Trying to catch what escapes me

But a moment too short

When will this fog clear?

Indefinitely caught between

Sanity

And

In

Side my thoughts

Captivated by the trance of chaos

Kept there

Haunted

Entrapped by myself

A POEM ABOUT THE SUN

BY OLIVIA SIMONE

They look up to the beauty that consumes us,

The heat that feeds us

Envelopes the Earth that they both

Cherish

And

Destroy.

When will she forgive us?

Will the Sun pray for us?

Bleed for us?

Die

For Us

Nothing feels right

It all feels wrong.

Just as I am, she is

Alone.

Always in sight

But always, always

Always

Out of reach.

I want her to know that we need her

That I love her

Her strength breathes down on Us

Seeping into our skin,

Our lives

And into our hearts

There blossoms

Her ephemeral grace

SHORT STORY

THE CASANOVA OF CÓRDOBA

BY ANTHONY MICHAEL PERRI

"I can't imagine being interested enough in somebody to do something about it". This was the maxim he lived by. It is what he would say to himself when he would get lost looking at himself in the mirror. From his small courtyard in the Juderia of Córdoba he would run his fingertips over and across the soft petals of the flowers, orchids hanging thick like sexual organs from the walls in his patio, a boudoir for one.

Through the skinny streets he sauntered, his fashion always in the height of style, close to the skin, hugging his body. His gait was stimulatingly feminine, simultaneously masculine, his composure strong and direct, with wide shoulders and rhythmic hips, in exactly equal parts, androgynously, unquestionably sexual, totally self-sufficient.

On Sundays, in the cathedral of the Mezquita, during a moment of silence dedicated to prayer, he would press his palms together close to his chest and delve deep into prayer.And while he would spare a passing word or two for his friends and family, he would pray most intensely and most sincerely for himself, caressing himself with his self-love, raising his heart up to God to ask for his benediction.

Afterwards, in the streets, the plazas, the cafés, he would flirt. Flirting was the most satisfying sport. Smiling at women and seducing them with his interesting choice of words. But only for the sense of pride. Only for the immaculate delight of being desirable.

Flirting was both the method and the completion of his social desires. He was only interested in the possibility of others. The concrete was dull. A temporary respite. A pursuit meant for the bajos, the general, the basic, a flavour for undeveloped palettes. What was built up in the fleeting glances, the soft touches, the clever innuendos, would be lost forever in an instant of sweaty exertion, and then all mystery would vanish, all possibility gone. His pursuits he deemed heavenly. He sought only the eternal.

Sparingly he would deign to lower himself into an engagement, for a few days, a week, a month at most. But these were always much more like trysts, silent affairs, forbidden for some irrelevant reason, scurried away in rented apartments, the dame bringing tea on platters between bouts. And even then, he would always be ethereal, coming and going, taking to the streets, never wanting to tie himself to anything. The only thing he could dedicate himself to, was himself.

He would buy himself chocolates and roses and take himself out to eat and see the sights, and treat himself to massages in the city baths and to shopping sprees in the market. His self-love infuriated those around him. He prayed he could be young and with himself forever.

He had a habit of resting his hand on his breast, a finger resting on his nipple. His arms would wrap around his body, he would caress himself. No one could please him like he could. Everyone else was a burden, a struggle, a bore and a chore.

The only concrete was himself.

The only thing he could tie himself too.

The only love eternal.

Forever engaged.

Until at last, his wish realized, his arms wrapped tight around his torso, his body became tight, like a straight-jacket in a madhouse, completely attached to himself, unable to move, unable to embrace anything, or anyone else...

LIFE WILL BE FILLED WITH NIGHTS LIKE THIS

BY TINA GIANG

I didn't know of the headwinds or the kind of world the rigid and unexplored path was going to lead my life into. And quite frankly, I was afraid that my silent voice was going to disappear without reaching anyone and fade away before my cries of help and wish for salvation could drip from my lips.

The memories of yesterday weighed me down. While, I struggled to move on from the regrets of today. But, I told myself to throw all my troubles and worries away and to just focus on what tomorrow will bring.

As the sunlight filtered through my thin and pale white curtains, they tenderly touched and healed my aching wounds. I laughed my regrets off because if yesterday couldn't touch me then why should I give it the chance to touch me today?

But then, night would arrive with its howling wind and its sharp fangs bared ready for an attack, it blew my thoughts into a whirlwind of complicated and unsolved emotions. It took me to a place that I believed that I had already escaped from. A place that I was all to familiar with. I seemed to be visiting it a lot more lately. It loves to creep up on me. It's an uninvited guest that had extended its stay, and refuses to leave. It doesn't have a home or a place to return to, so it decides to make a home in me instead. How bothersome. I felt all alone, empty, wary, hesitant and vulnerable.

So, I gazed up at the milky moon and asked for her to give me reassurance and hope. I told her that, 'Despite knowing the headwinds and hardships ahead, I know that isn't an excuse or a reason to stop me from going forward. I thought that all I wanted out of life was maybe just to grow old for the sake of it. But I no longer want that. I have no desire for that anymore. I want to live! To live! I just want to live! To live for my family, for my friends, for my dreams or better yet, for myself! I want to find that recipe for a long life. I want to find the ingredients that is needed to make that sweet and delectable elixir. The sweetness and bitterness of life. A bittersweet elixir. The taste of life itself.' She whispered to me to throw away the things that I had grown attached to, had embraced and had been stuck with.

Once, I could let go of the things that had weighed my body, my mind, my heart and my soul down, I felt free and was able to start my life anew. But as humans, nights like these are common and hard to escape from so I tell them to her, the moon, and asked her to give me the courage to face them once again. I entrust her with them, my abandoned and forgotten dreams, my unanswered thoughts and my wishes so that I'll be able to overcome this night, and face a new and different tomorrow.

AN OLD FASHIONED

BY MADISON LIPSKY

I gently slice off the orange peel, careful not to accidentally catch my finger in the projected direction of the blade. I muddle the orange peel in the big clear glass with some simple syrup and precisely four dashes of orange bitters. I can smell the zest and tang from above the mixing glass. It has come to the most important part; I add 2.5 ounces of strong Bourbon Whiskey to the mixing glass. My nose tingles when it gets its sudden whiff of Bourbon. It makes me wince for a second but ultimately makes me want to take a swig of it myself. I mix it up with ice and then pour the mixed drink over a fancier glass with exactly one rock of ice. I peel another orange, squeeze it into the drink, then drop it in before giving it one last swirl. Wala... an old fashioned.

I hand over the carefully made drink to the man that sits in front of me. He is wearing a plain business suit and his hair is messy as if he has been grasping onto it in moments of stress and despair. It seems to me this man is tired, upset, and overly run down from the brutal streak of life's unexpected miseries. Usually, a businessperson who orders an old-fashioned before 5 P.M. shares this feeling of grief and stress. As I gently slide the drink towards him, I give him a warm smile, maybe it will brighten his day.

As a bartender, my job doesn't start and end with preparing drinks for customers. It is much more complex than that. My job as revolves around understanding and connecting with humanity. I am there for the ones who come in sad, the ones who celebrate, the ones who recently had an incredibly drastic change in their lives, good or bad. I am their confidant, a listener, and in some cases a guide who shares my advice with the people that need it. I take immense pride in what I do because as I learn about the people, I encounter I also learn a little more about myself along the way.

When the businessman meets my smiling eyes he gives me a nod, holds up his drink and makes a cheers. He cheers to his youngest son getting married in the upcoming weekend. Maybe my judgment was wrong. I begin talking with him, getting to know the ins and outs of his son's very special day. Even though this man seems excited for his son I still cannot shake the feeling of the despair that is radiating around him. He eventually transitions into sharing with me the story of him and his wife's beautiful marriage. They have been married for 15 years. I say congratulations with astonishment as successful marriages seem to be rare through a bartender's eyes who serves a lot of alcoholics and lost people. He doesn't talk about his wedding day, instead he talks with great passion about their honeymoon that followed. They went to Ireland for five days and re-fell in love with each other like it was the first time.

The man is almost done his drink, he takes one last swig, sets the whiskey glass on the bar, and looks at me. He asks me if he can give me a piece of advice. I nod as if to say, go ahead. He says, "If you ever want to get married, don't have a big extravagant wedding, honestly don't even have the reception!" I look at him in awe and intrigue, motioning for him to continue. It seems that what he has to say, he has been holding in for quite some time. "I remember one thing about my wedding day, just stress. It was not a magical day for me or my beautiful wife to enjoy. It was a time to please our guests, to make sure everything went perfectly. If I had to go back in time, we would have had eloped in a court room, then spent all the money we wasted on our wedding and traveled for a month or two in the beautiful land of Ireland, maybe even around Europe. That's what would've made me and my wife the happiest." I look at him with respect for admitting something many people do not agree with nor see eye to eye on. It makes me consider the day in which I get married, maybe I should take this man's advice. I ask him if he told his son what he had just told me. He says, "Yes, but my son never listens to me." He sets down his drink, puts a $20 bill on the counter, giving me a 30% tip. "He never has and never will." He sighs, gives me a wave and a nod and then leaves.

A few hours pass and three pretty young ladies in their late 20's, early 30's enter the bar. They are being quite loud and rambunctious. I have a feeling they are celebrating a change within one of their lives. I go over to their lively energy. "What can I get you ladies?" They look at me with big grins and overwhelming excitement. "Champagne!!!" one of the women say. "Coming right up!" I grab three extravagant champagne glasses, pop open the bubbly, and begin to pour being careful to ensure the fizz does not overflow. "What are we celebrating?" I ask intrigued by their overwhelming energy and joy. "I finally moved into my new apartment today!!" The one woman exclaims with great pride. "Congratulations!!" I say. I pour myself a glass of the fine champaign too. I could not help it; their energy is intoxicating and overly contagious. We cheer for a new beginning.

Later that night the local hippie comes in. I serve him three to four times per week. He always gets the same three glasses of Cabernet 9 oz. pour each time. He is in his late 60's and always wears his Tye dye T-shirt and dirt brown sandals, no matter what the weather. I find his stories very interesting as they are unlike stories I've never heard before. By his third glass of red wine, he begins to say outrageous things about life in general. Whether that be his belief of aliens and extraterrestrial life, or the existence of bigfoot and mermaids, to the study of drugs and narcotics. He is always sharing with me some crazy ideas and grants me with wild conversations. Usually the conversations are one sided, I let him talk for hours while I just listen in awe of his unique personality. Today he talks to me about recarnation. He believes in his next life that he will be an aquatic animal, not a human. He tells me that life is not fair and we can't control the life we have been dealt with since it was decided for us since birth. I listen to his words and nod and smile as I always do. This time I interject and tell him that in my next life I will be a famous soccer player from Madrid. I do not believe in recarnation but I do believe in the power of out of the box conversation, expanding one's minds by the influence of other people's beliefs.

Approximately thirty minuets before closing a young women enters with tear soaked eyes. She sits at the bar and does not speak a word except for "a shot of Whiskey." I pour her a glass and ask if she's all right. Her strong barrier of resistance to speaking gets torn down as she begins to pour her heart and soul out to me. She tells me about her recent heartbreak, I comfort her by sharing stories of my previous heart breaks. At one point we are both crying to one another. Sometimes two broken hearts can heal each other.

When I clock out of my shift at 12:00 AM my feet ache, my joints scream for rest, but my mind and heart feel full. Human interaction is crucial to human fulfillment. A job in which I get to share the experience of life with others is all I have dreamt of. An old fashioned is not just a mixed drink consisting of bourbon whiskey, it's a measurement of time, the amount of time it takes for one human to connect with another.

FINDING CLOSURE

BY ZARA MENHENNET

Pulling on the hand break, Sarah eyed the darkening skies, the grey carpet rolled out for her arrival. It was over a decade since her last visit to the coast, and leaning back in her seat, she gazed out to sea. Clouds eclipsing the sun, the sparkle faded, just as it had in her marriage. Meanwhile, getting impatient in the back, Calypso whined and scuffed about, lining the upholstery with her black fur. Heaving a sigh, Sarah unbuckled herself and stepped out into the bitter afternoon breeze.

'Hang on, you dopey creature. If you don't stop wriggling, I'll never attach this!'

Clipping the collar, Sarah pulled the black labrador from the back seat, and making a quick check for poo bags, walked over to the parking meter.

'Scandalous,' she muttered, pulling out a couple of pounds.

Ticket in hand, she stuck it inside her windscreen and pocketing a few sweets, closed the door. Fighting loose strands of hair out of her face and zipping her jacket to the top, she pulled Calypso in tight and headed for the sloping ramp that led into the bay.

Her divorce was now official, but she was still battling to come to terms with what had happened. It wasn't his affairs, those she had discovered were fleeting and numerous.Rather, it was his falling out of love with her that she found hard. They had known each other for over fifteen years before they had married, having met at this very beach. Dorset had never been home to her, but ever since her first holiday with her parents, it held a special place in her wounded heart.

Playing with her ring on her finger, she stopped and breathed in the salty spray that circulated the inlet. Nearly a complete circle, the cove was well protected, its small entrance guarded by the rocky slopes leading away on each side. It was deserted, unlike her first visit all those years ago, and unclicking Calypso's lead, she let her off to run free.

Plunging her hands into her pockets, Sarah walked out into the openness of the cove, pebbles lining the crescent beach. Screwing up her face, she moaned inwardly as Calypso went paddling – well there was no stopping her now, and smiling to herself, she stepped out onto the stones to join her.

'Where you going?' she called, 'Calypso!' Oh well, she never went far. Besides, if Sarah gave the liver treats a quick shake, Calypso would be back in a heartbeat. 'Calypso, come here girl!'

Examining the high cliffs, her green eyes looked upwards. The grey had progressively evolved into a sombre black, promising an imminent downpour.

'Calypso!Come back!' she shouted, as the black tail continued to waggle further along the shoreline. 'Damn it, what's she seen? Calypso!'

Grumbling, Sarah trudged angrily along the water's edge. Despite its narrow inlet, the waters were forming small crests and the wind now whipped her cheeks. Shaking the bag again, she tried in vain to recall the dog, who seemed oblivious to her owner's cries. Honestly, what had she seen? Clenching the lead, Sarah suddenly stopped. There, further around the curve, she could make out the figure of somebody crouching near the water.

'Calypso!' she shouted into the wind. 'Calypso, stop!'

The dog stopped abruptly, but showed no intention of returning. Sarah was almost beside her when she looked ahead at the figure that remained crouched by the water. A little way off, but close enough to make out, Sarah wrinkled her nose at the smell of rotting fish. A smell that recalled a horrifying memory...

Sarah's chest tightened, her knuckles turning white as she gripped the bag of treats.She recognised that figure squatting beside the water. She shivered as a fear clawed at her base of her neck and her hairs stood on end. She felt cold, a chill that had nothing to do with the droplets now falling from the heavens. Beside her, Calypso had started to growl, a low and steady beat that echoed from her throat. Transfixed, her legs turned to lead as she stared at the figure that crouched in the same spot as twenty years ago, the same day she had met James.

She was only ten years old when her parents had brought her here on holiday, the first of many that would lead to her future life. Her mind flashed as the memory surfaced, gleaming as if it were only yesterday...

'Don't go far, Sarah. It looks like rain.'

'Yes, mum, but just a little more,' she nagged.

'Ten minutes and then we're going.'

Jumping up, Sarah ran along the beach, the pebbles giving way beneath her jelly shoes.What were a few black clouds anyway?

Relishing every second, she splashed and kicked as she danced along the shore, her parents packing up their picnic. However, it wasn't long before she felt puffed and slowing to draw breath, she tilted her head back, feeling the drizzle against her skin. She was just turning to go back when a figure caught her eye, crouched by the water. It looked like a boy, no more than seven or eight, and his clothes were tatty and sodden through.

'Hello?' called Sarah, but the boy didn't answer. 'Hello? Are you okay?'. Still no answer.

Unsure, Sarah looked back towards her parents. Where were they? She couldn't see them. In fact, she saw nobody! They hadn't left without her? Panicking, she looked up towards the rocky hillside when...what was that smell? A pungent mix of rotting fish and...and...she didn't know, but it smelt awful. Glancing back to the crouching boy, she let out a startled cry. He had moved closer and was now no more than a few meters away.

Her heart pounded against her swimsuit and the hairs on her arms stood on end as a chill coursed its way up her neck. She was transfixed, unable to move her legs.

'Who are you?' she whispered.

The boy made no reply, but continued to play, cupping something out of sight, twisting his wrists and dipping his hands into the water. His fingers were long and spindly, their ends tipped with nails that appeared uncut for some time. Her eyes travelled along his sleeves to his pale neck, where his black hair stuck, wet and entangled with seaweed. High cheekbones formed a gaunt profile to which Sarah felt a strong sense of unease.Suddenly, the pebbles shifted beneath her shoes, causing the boy to start, his face turning to hers. Letting out a shriek, she stumbled backwards.

'What?' he sneered, his lips curling back to reveal a set of filed teeth. 'You've wondered too far today, should've listened to mummy.' His eyes flashed dangerously, a brilliant amber, streaked with copper that made way to a quickly dilating black slit.

'Wh-what are you?' she wheezed.

'What am I?You mean, what are you? Besides being a naughty girl that has come into my realm. This is my cove, not yours and always has been. So, if I decide to defend it,' he snarled, 'I have every right.'

The rain was falling heavily now, her auburn hair strangling her neck. Sarah's eyes flicked between those that met hers and his clawed hands that hid something that shone with astounding brilliance.

'It's mine,' he whispered, eyeing her closely. 'The sun is mine to keep. It always rains in the cove and visitors are not welcome here.'

Sarah had seen enough. She was scared and wanted to find her parents.

'You think that is possible now?' sniggered the boy.

'What?I didn't say anything.'

'Didn't have to. I know what you want to do, and the answer is no.' Sarah gulped; he had read her thoughts! She wanted to get out of there, but she had lost all strength in her legs. 'Besides,' he went on, 'it must be around teatime, and I am ever so hungry for something fresh.'

Letting out a scream, Sarah made to run away, but slipping on some slimy pebbles landed hard upon the sand. Panic overtook her as she tried to scramble to her feet. Meanwhile, the boy twisted his body towards her, and pocketing its treasure, a crooked smiled spread across his face.

'Come now, you are just making it more difficult for me to drag you under,' he cooed, wrapping his fingers around her one ankle. 'Time to go.'

Taking hold of her other ankle he tugged her legs across the sand. Grip tight, he stumbled, suddenly unable to drag her further.What was stopping him? Sarah had felt it too, a tug had been made in another direction, from her wrist. Then, she felt it again! She was being pulled in the opposite direction by a different set of hands. Human hands.

'Help me, please!' she cried to her invisible rescuer.

'You're mine,' snarled the boy, tugging hard towards the rough sea. She cried as her ankle twisted in his clasp, a plain that shot up to the knee. 'No!You're mine!' He shouted against the invisible enemy.

But as Sarah looked back, she saw the creature fade from sight, its grip lost and the sun blinding her.

'Are you okay?' asked a voice. 'Hello.Can you hear me?'

She nodded.The voice was warm and comforting, a boy's voice. Blinking, she shielded her eyes from the sun as a face hovered above hers, hazel eyes staring at her from above a freckled nose.

'You okay?I'm James.'

Her love, James, had saved her all those years ago from the very creature that now crouched once more before her and Calypso. Watching, she saw that the boy again cupped something in its hands, a dull shine of gold. Taking a ginger step back, she tried to retreat unseen, but the boy froze, turning its face towards hers.

'It's been a long time,' the boy whispered. Sarah's heart pounded in her ears, drowning out Calypso's growl beside her. 'And you brought company,' he smiled, playfully snapped his jaws at the dog.

With a whimper, Calypso retreated behind, the last of her valour spent. Sarah had never taken Calypso to be much of a guard dog, but had hoped that in a moment of crisis she may have proved worthy.

'Ha-ha.Your little doggy is not going to save you today. But having said that...nor is James.' The boy paused, holding out his hand to the water in front of him. 'I believe this belongs to you,' he continued, unfolding his fingers to reveal a golden ring.

Sarah stifled a cry and looked at her hand. Her wedding ring had gone! All that remained was a faded white line.

'How did you -'

'It's time, Sarah, to say goodbye to him. He may have saved you that day but perhaps he delivered you into a worse place.'

'That's not true.'

'He doesn't love you.'

'What would you know?'

'It is here in this ring. It does not glow with the beauty of the sun that it once did, the day that he rescued you.'

Sarah stared, her heart paining. What did this all mean? Had she returned to the place she met James just to die? A final collapse of marriage and life?

'No, you haven't', the boy replied to her thoughts, 'you have come to find closure.Love without sunlight will not flourish and nor will you. To leave this realm of mine, where the sun does not shine, either you or the ring must stay behind.'

Tears welled in her eyes as her life with James seemed to wash away with the waves at her feet. It was over, where it had all begun. She closed her eyes, turning her face to the falling rain, but felt nothing against her skin. She blinked, shielding her eyes from the sun that shone above. Looking about hurriedly, she found Calypso sat beside her, and looking down at her hand, she saw that her ring was gone.

WHY THE VOLCANO ERUPTS

BY GABRIELLA HARRISON

Many years ago, there was a fierce battle between a god and a human man for the hand of an exceedingly beautiful maiden. The god was affronted by the audacity of the human to compete with him. The human although knowing what he was doing was dangerous, was so smitten with the beautiful maiden, he didn't care what the consequence would be to him or to his fellow humans.

The competition went on for so long and became so violent, that the maiden had to intervene. She finally gave them a quest. They had seven days to bring her a rare treasure never seen by anyone and difficult to get, and the person who could accomplish this would have her hand. The god laughed and went away confident he would achieve this before the seven days. Meanwhile, the human felt dismayed. He knew how powerful the god was and that he had access to an abundance of treasures in Olympus-where he dwelled. He started to feel defeated.

The human man loved the beautiful maiden so much. There had to be something he could do. He became determined not to lose to the god who had an unfair advantage. He sat by the stream and pondered on how he could win the challenge. What could he possibly get from the earth that would impress the maiden and that has never been seen before? As he stared into the beautiful and clear stream he noticed the far mountains reflected in the stream and they reminded him of The Volcanos of Hera.

Surely, he wouldn't dare. The Volcanos of Hera were known to be extremely dangerous, men and even gods avoided it. The Volcanos hate being disturbed, and they swallow those who dare disturb them. Many have gone in search of its treasures, and secrets, but have never returned. His desperation and the love he had for the maiden soon clouded his logic. He decided that he had to travel to The Volcanos of Hera, as it would be the perfect place to get a gem so rare and never seen by anyone. He knew his mission was very risky and he might not return. But if he could successfully return, the maiden would not only be impressed by his gift but also by his courage and the tales he would bring back.

All men would adore him, and it wouldn't matter that he wasn't a god, even the gods would want to hear how he achieved such a great fit. Yes, he had to do this. He must go to The Volcanos of Hera.

The next day, he packed all he would need and set off for the volcanos. Getting there was no easy fit, he faced many challenges. He had to outsmart talking trees, disappearing paths, swift weather changes, shaking grounds, and sleep in a tree to escape wild animals. Even with all these obstacles, he kept going determined not to fail. On the fourth day, he finally reached the volcanos.

Fear started creeping in as he stood before the mighty Volcanos of Hera. He resolved that he had come this far, so he would proceed even as The Volcanos of Hera and the ground started shaking. The unsteady ground made it difficult for him to approach. Finally, he got to the entrance of the volcano, and he cautiously entered. To his surprise everywhere became still, the ground ceased its shaking, and there was silence.

He looked around him in awe, in every direction it glowed. In his amazement and excitement, he began to jump and shout. This would be easy he thought, and he eagerly rushed in to explore the volcano's contents. While doing this, he saw a part of it that shone brighter than the other sides, and it changed colors. In wonder, he decided to break a chunk off. As he proceeded to do this, he heard a loud and thundering voice. "Who dares to disturb the Volcanos of Hera." He immediately began to tremble as the ground shook, and he looked all around him but saw no one. Hello, who's there? He called out. The same thundering voice replied, "The Volcanos of Hera demand to know who is the invader that has dared to disturb the peace we have enjoyed for years."

The poor and afraid human told the voice his plight and how much he loved the beautiful maiden. The voice listened intently and when he was done said he could take anything he wanted. He was so overjoyed, he thanked the voice and began choosing precious stones and various gems and treasures that were never before seen by anyone. When he finished gathering, he prepared to leave when the same voice stopped him. There was one condition.

He could take anything he wanted, but he must never return to the human world. The human became sorrowful. He loved the maiden so much and wanted to please her and win her love, but he couldn't bear to never see her again. The thought of returning and seeing her with the god forever and being a source of mockery in the town was even more disturbing. He wouldn't be able to stand seeing her with anyone else or to see the look of disappointment in her eyes. So he agreed. The gems would be sent to her and his sacrifice and courage would be told to her.

He sent her a message expressing his love for her, and hope that they would one day meet again. When the maiden received his message and his gifts, she was overcome with so much emotion. The gifts from the god soon turned to rubbish before her eyes. This human had sacrificed much more; he had sacrificed his life out of love for her. She declared him the winner and vowed to mourn and remember him forever. From time to time she would go to cry on volcanos in remembrance of him. In response to her tears and their love, the volcanos would erupt.

Contact us

You can contact Hermes Magazine in these ways.

Email:
Hermesmagazinelondon@yahoo.com

LinkedIn:
www.linkedin.com/company/hermesmagazine

Website:
www.hermesmagazine.yolasite.com